There is no "formula"  one trait stands out a grace to engage God's tity. Who He is, and who He created each of us to be. Sean Harvey understands this as one who truly has been formed in secret. In this timely book, he shares many Biblical truths that spring to life when described by a man clearly overtaken by the love and affection of his heavenly Father through all of life's circumstances. Every time I read, I am more encouraged in my understanding of God's sovereign plan, and my created value. You will be too!

—MIKE MASSÉ
PASTOR AND AUTHOR OF #IAMHOLY

Formed in Secret will take you on a journey of spiritual transformation as you experience the passion and transparency of Sean's walk with the Lord. It will challenge you to think outside of the box called religion and cause you to dig deeper into the areas of your life that have been held captive. Sean's story will inspire you to live a life surrendered to the Lover of your soul and will ignite your heart to be consumed by the only relationship that can unlock your God-given identity.

—CINDI KORMAN
PASTORAL CARE AND DELIVERANCE MINISTRY
KING OF KINGS WORSHIP CENTER
BASKING RIDGE, NJ

This book will help you find freedom and joy! One of the things that should be obvious about God is that He is extraordinarily creative. And His creation is so diverse that not even two snowflakes are alike. So it should go without saying that every human being is unique. Yet, we are told that every human being is created to be an image bearer of God Himself. How can we be different and unique, yet at the same time, each bear the image of the one true God? Read Sean's journey as he discovered the answer to these questions in Jesus Christ. Let the insights from his journey encourage your own journey to discover the riches of life in Jesus.

—WESTON BROOKS
LEAD PASTOR
RIVER OF LIFE CHRISTIAN FELLOWSHIP
TOLLAND, CT

Grab a cup of coffee and pull up a chair because you are going to be here a while. At least I was: not once, but twice. Much like a modern day Gene Edwards, Sean will captivate you as he delicately brings you into his story while simultaneously helping you realize your own. With the gentle heart of a shepherd, he will help you unwind some of the mysteries and secrets you have been longing to discover—not really about yourself, but about your heavenly Father. I am so amazed at the depth of my dear friend, Sean, and can truly say this book has impacted my life.

—RANDY GOUDEAU, JR.
YOUTH LEADER AND REVIVALIST
FORT SMITH, AZ

FORMED
IN SECRET

SEAN D. HARVEY

CREATION
HOUSE

Library of Congress Cataloging in Publication Data:
2015939486
International Standard Book Number: 978-1-62998-449-0
E-book International Standard Book Number:
978-1-62998-450-6

While the author has made every effort to provide accurate
telephone numbers and Internet addresses at the time of
publication, neither the publisher nor the author assumes
any responsibility for errors or for changes that occur after
publication.

First edition

15 16 17 18 19—987654321
Printed in the United States of America

CONTENTS

Acknowledgments ix

Introduction xi

Chapter 1: An Open Door 1

Chapter 2: Hearts of Stone 7

Chapter 3: Created for Love 15

Chapter 4: In the Image and Likeness 21

Chapter 5: The Inner Place 27

Chapter 6: Sharing in Glory 31

Chapter 7: All Consuming Fire .35

Chapter 8: Becoming You 41

Chapter 9: Choosing to be Known 47

Chapter 10: The Cost of Freedom 53

Chapter 11: The Need for Freedom 63

Chapter 12: Choosing Freedom .69

Chapter 13: The Baseline 77

Chapter 14: Exposed by the Holy Spirit 85

Chapter 15: Engaging Love 97

Chapter 16: Access to God 105

Simply God 111

About the Author 113

Contact the Author 114

ACKNOWLEDGMENTS

N O ONE WALKS ALONE. THE RELEASE OF this book, this snapshot discussion of how God is revealing in me who I was created to be, has been not only my journey, but the paths of many lives that have altered my life forever.

To my beloved wife Jessica, the woman whose heart calls my heart to be all that I am: thank you, my Love, for always believing the best about me and being my constant reminder of how God sees me. This book is as much yours as mine.

To my mom and dad, whose lives taught me to never give up, to always fight for what I believe in, and to embrace my dreams without apologizing for how crazy they look to others: thank you for being you. Your courage has always inspired me to keep reaching into the wild!

To my brothers in adoption, who have fought by my side like the Mighty Men—only God knows the broken man I would be without your unwavering love and willingness to journey with me through the darkest nights. I am who I am today because of each of you. You know who you are.

Thank you to the pastors who have faithfully

shepherded my soul over the years, wherever God led me: Bruce Morgan, Sam Lee, Chris Ho, Peter and Trisha Roselle, Cindi Korman, Easter Frazier, Jeremy Burden, and Weston Brooks: You have each added wisdom and honor to my story.

Thank you to Weston Brooks and Cindi Korman, whose feedback on content and Biblical truth made this book so much more than I could have made it alone.

Thank you to Mike Massé, who introduced me to Creation House, and has been my creative soundboard through this whole process.

Thank you to Ken and Teri Vaughn for believing in Jess and I, and for believing that God has something to say to people through the words of this book. You are priceless in His Kingdom!

Thank you to everyone whose financial contributions have made this book possible. It would still be a file on my hard drive without all of you.

Thank you to all who have walked with me. In each one of you I have seen more of who God is—infinitely beautiful and full of love.

INTRODUCTION

May 9, 2013

I WAS HAVING DINNER WITH MY ROOMMATE one evening a couple of years ago. We sat in the restaurant, him with a salad and me with a burrito. We were talking, as we usually did, about the many facets of relationships. He was engaged to be married, and my marriage had recently come to a long and painful end. I had made some goofy joke, and while I was laughing and he was shaking his head at me, he asked how my goofy sense of humor played out in my marriage. It was a good question, and I said, "It didn't really fit in well.'" It was a common answer I gave regarding my marriage— that though I may have been loved, I seldom felt really enjoyed.

And then he asked the perfect question. It really cut to the heart of my life for the nearly ten years of marriage, and moreover, my life as a whole. It spoke to the core of my life from day one, my life as I have lived it, and how all the choices I make add up to the life that is expressed through me. He asked just the right question: "Bro... who were you?"

To me it was not just a question about my marriage. It is not even a question I had to answer before moving into a new relationship. It is the question that sits at the very foundation of my life—and not only my life, but it is the bottom line of each individual life: "who are you?" The answer to that question defines us in a way that no other answer does, and it is not an easy question to answer. It is simultaneously the question that challenges our lives as we have lived them, and also the answer that determines what future will take shape by the choices that express our lives. This question is at the core of each and every person.

Am I the person "they" say I am? Should I be the person "they" say I should be? Am I the person I say I am, and should I even be the one to define my true identity? Will I choose to take a hard and fast stand for who I am regardless of what anyone thinks of me, or will I warp and twist myself to fit some unknown and shifting standard? These are the kinds of questions that operate in every person, whether we realize it or not. And whether we process the question and come up with an answer or not, there is *always* an answer. Somewhere hidden in the belly of our lives there is an answer that defines our being. We are full of that answer, whatever it is.

The really big question is, "Who is answering that question?" Do the people who have answered our question, the ones who have defined us, know us at all? Have they taken the time to see us, hear us, walk through life with us? Do they know the very fabric of our beings? Do we? Most likely, they do not, and we don't either. We have been so conditioned throughout our lives to accept certain facts that they have become indelible truths to our minds. I think if we really considered these questions, we would find that most of us have been defined so absolutely and yet so unintentionally. There has been very little effort made by those around us to define us accurately, and despite our best efforts, we typically fall short in discovering ourselves also.

The hope we have is that there is a way to unlock true identity. It is to discover that there is only One who has the information necessary, the passion required, the innate perseverance that not only breaks down the false but raises up what is true in us. God alone, the One who made each and every one of us, knows the plan and purpose of each person. He has not only an understanding of the destiny of our lives but the blueprint of our very being. He is solely knowledgeable as to who we were made to be and how we live from the place of design and destiny, and not simply out of our efforts to survive. He is the only one who really knows us and who can show us the way to ourselves. It is only through Him that we can come face to face with the person only He knows we are to be.

It is God's greatest desire and joy to reveal in us, and to us, the person we were intended to be from the first word of creation. It is through knowing God and being known by Him that we are completely unveiled. It is in that place of love that we are made completely new, completely whole, completely alive, and completely ourselves.

Chapter 1

AN OPEN DOOR

TRUE LIFE BEGINS AT THE CROSS. THE CROSS is the door, the entry, and though it is one we must pass through many times daily, it is not the destination. Jesus declares, "I am the resurrection and the life. The one who believes in me will live, even though they die..." (John 11:25). Jesus never says that He is the death we need. He is the life we must have. He is the restoration of everything that we were made to be. He did not come to usurp our beings and produce a vast population of identically operational entities. He came to release in us the person we were designed to be—the fullness of the expression of God that each of us was intended to reveal from the foundation of the world. He planned each one of us to be a certain way, with our own gifts, talents, smiles, hands, and unique expressions. That is what He gave everything for, and what we must give everything to have. We must let Jesus in to accomplish the work of showing us not only the way to Himself, but the way through Him, to ourselves.

It is not selfish to be the person you were created to be. It is only self-indulgent if you let that become your whole purpose, or act as if God was only interested in you. God's intention is to expose the truest expression of who you are as a way to reveal the truest expression of who He is to you, and through you, and in doing so build a relationship with you that will pour over the people who are touched by your life.

I am a passionate, talkative, curious person with a huge appetite for learning and a corny sense of humor. Those are some of my qualities. That would not describe a lot of people. Some for sure, but not everyone—and it would be a far more boring place on earth if everyone was like me. It would also be extremely out of order. I can be far too passionate sometimes and over excitable. It has made me rash and unthinking at times, and I am grateful for the people in my life that are nothing like me that God has used to challenge me and encourage me to look at the other aspects of a situation, and life as a whole.

People need to be looked at the same way. It is best when we see the many aspects of people. It is necessary for all of us to see and appreciate the differences in others. Sometimes it is extremely difficult to desire these differences, but without them, we will ultimately see God less also. We have the opportunity to express and know the varied aspects of an infinite God. Without each other we will know Him less, enjoy Him less, and by neglecting each other we neglect the great joy He takes in us.

So we come back to the cross. It is at the cross that we lay down our preconceptions, our judgments, our fears and the all-to-easy rejection of those we do not understand. It is at the cross we have the opportunity to choose a life that flows from God into us and shows us the importance of life as He intended it. He will show us the value of the others He has made, why they were made, and how they can open us up to knowing Him. It is at the cross that we can surrender our identity to Jesus so He can reveal to us our truest identity through His full understanding of how we were intended to be at creation.

Without Jesus, we take our misconceived identities with us into every relationship we have. Usually the people we choose to open up to help us to know our own weaknesses first. I have seen my greatest sins with alarming clarity in my closest relationships, and have really seen my capacity to hold others away from me. Most of us never realize how distant we keep people from us. For me it took quite some time to see because I am willing to share just about anything, and I tend to admit that I am wrong very easily. However, I was not seeing the walls around me keeping people at bay. From the outside it may have looked like I was an open book, but internally I was a walled city. What I was hiding were all the thoughts that revealed my fears, my insecurities, and my inability to trust. Most of us do this in some way, perhaps not with the same issues, but with something. And despite how well I thought I was hiding them, they were very apparent to those who know me best.

Often we create a world that looks like intimacy but never really open the door. We are familiar with all the devices that signify real love, but it may be that we have never really experienced love. We create a world that exists only like a movie. It can be turned on and turned off, paused or put in slow motion. We put on a great show, but it is not creating anything lasting and real. A good many of us don't really know how to have a conversation without putting on a good performance for others while having a whole different story playing out in our minds.

What Jesus offers is a way to end the show. For me it has been a slow and deliberate process of breaking one path after another of thought and action. Holy Spirit comes and touches one thought at a time, unraveling the falsehood in my mind and revealing the truth that would replace those empty plans. Purposefully, tenaciously, He speaks to each aspect and area of my life that needs to be restored to the design of creation, and all the while, His plan is to reveal me to myself. He cannot inhabit a structure of lies and selfishness, so He brings an end to everything that does not have real life in it. Then He fills it with Life.

The filling aspect is the real key and is what freedom is really based on. Dying to self, carrying our cross daily, making sacrifices is all about entering a place where Jesus lives. When we are willing to face death, we are ready to be trusted with life. That is the big plan. Jesus wants to give life away, more and more and more of it. He is so excited to pass His life on, but the dead cannot have life or give it, so we must pass through death—where we are actually living anyway—to where He is. He is the God of the living, not the dead, and He is living free.

I have found one of the greatest challenges is to stop focusing on not sinning and remember to focus on love. The more I try to not sin, to omit something from my life, the harder I find it to accomplish. This is because my mind is on sin, not on life. But we are exhorted to focus on "whatever is true, whatever is noble, whatever is right, whatever is pure, whatever is lovely, whatever is admirable—if anything is excellent or praiseworthy—think about such things"(Phil. 4:8). I am in no way talking about the power of positive thinking. I am talking about being full of power because we are full of God's life. It is part of the original design, and so it is what we are made to be.

Jesus gave everything for us to be restored to the life He designed and created us to have. The cost of having it is surrendering everything we have designed and created to cover up the absence of His life in us. The cost is dropping the fig leaves and standing in front of God naked, saying, "I was trying to cover up my shame at being separate from You. I am terrified at the absence of your love. I just want you to show me who I am made to be."

I can only say that being vulnerable with God is worth doing, and really needs to be done if we are to have relationship with Him. Walking it out has been the most difficult challenge I have ever faced in my life. I have been angry with God, screaming and yelling and full of hate. I have fallen and failed and wallowed in self-pity many times, only to have Him gently take me by the arm, tell me how proud He is of me, and give me the strength to rise and keep on going. It has been a journey beyond my expression, in both wonder and joy as well as heartache and loss. I would not exchange it for anything.

Chapter 2

HEARTS OF STONE

PERHAPS THE GREATEST SINGLE HINDRANCE to everything that Jesus wants to share with us is religion. What I mean when I say religion is everything that removes the unique, special, and perfect differences that mark each of us as a creation of God. Religion puts upon us the weight of measures rather than the weight of glory, but all creation longs to be "brought into the freedom and glory of the children of God" (Rom. 8:21). God made us to reveal Himself, to reflect His true being, His ways, His beauty, and His limitlessness. When we are being who He made us to be, we show off the vast and intricate expressions of our living God. If we live under the burden of being something other than ourselves, we find very quickly we are exhausted, confused, and lack the passion that defines a life in God. We were not made for religion but for relationship.

Religion is really a show that attempts to make others comfortable. It is a template people use on themselves and others so that judgment is made easier. It is a measuring line for man rather than a plumb line used by God. Religion exemplifies the fallen nature in that it has everything to do with the knowledge of good and evil rather than the knowledge of God. It has no relationship with the Lord, no love for Jesus, no compassion for others, and no mercy for anyone. Religion is relentless and strives to keep you bound to the lies that create every wrong idea we have about who we are. It wants us to believe that man was created evil by nature. But God, by nature, is calling to us with freedom, saying, "Come to me! Come home."

The book of Isaiah sums it up very simply. "…God will speak to this people, to whom He said, 'This is the resting place, let the weary rest'; and, 'This is the place of repose'—but they would not listen. So then, the word of the Lord to them will become: Do this, do that, a rule for this, a rule for that; a little here, a little there—so that as they go they will fall backward; they will be injured and snared and captured" (Isa. 28:11–13). To be bound to a life of endless rules and work is not God's desire for us. It is not His first offer to us to be injured, snared, and captured. It is only if we do not receive His free offer that He be our place of rest and repose that we will then be subjected to the consequences of separation: do and do until we fall backwards and get injured. This is the result of our choice, not His. He is simply letting us know that the result of rejecting Him leads to a life of religion, which leads to captivity.

Isaiah goes on to say in verse 15 that to avoid the consequences of their rejection of God they "made a lie [their] refuge and falsehood [their] hiding place." They create a false identity to hide their vulnerability. First they choose to reject God's offer of peace through relationship. Then, when the world comes against them, they "made an agreement...with death" to hide from destruction. They are hiding from destruction by asking death to cover over their inability to protect themselves. Do I need to say that death cannot save your life? Okay good. So, what does God say to this? "...See, I lay a stone in Zion, a tested stone, a precious cornerstone for a sure foundation; the one who trusts will never be dismayed. I will make justice the measuring line and righteousness the plumb line..." (Isa. 28:16–17). He speaks of Jesus, the Cornerstone. He reminds us that despite the failure of our own efforts, even when we have rejected Him, we can turn to Jesus to find an identity that comes from "the place of repose."

God is showing us that He is more interested in the heart of a person than the outward appearance of righteousness. He is saying that Jesus is the true Measure of justice and the true Revealer of the upright. If there are two things that Jesus really focused on while He was bodily on the earth, it was the healing and restoration of the broken and the confrontation of religion. He was continually challenging the religious leaders about their attitude toward righteousness, the uselessness of their efforts for their own sake, and the burden placed on others by their hardened requirements for the outward representation of a good life. Jesus made, and makes, a personal agenda of breaking the identity of religion over the lives of people and revealing how He desires to take us in and give us rest. Can we agree that it is more restful to live a life being yourself than trying to measure up? Jesus comes to show that we face others and ourselves with kindness, because kindness leads us to repentance, and repentance leads to new ways of thinking and seeing (Rom. 2:4).

Religion had its start with the first lie in Eden. It has emerged from the lie the serpent told Eve, convincing her that when God made her and Adam, He had withheld something from them that they needed. Religion tells us that we need to have something that is not from God. It seeks to separate. It makes dividing lines that say one is better than another based on their actions: if you do this thing you are good, and if you do that thing, you are bad. Yet in reality it is not even the rule that creates religion, but the hard use of the rule by those who do not understand grace and mercy. Religion is the result of applying rules apart from the life of the Ruler.

The truth is there is no action that makes us either better or worse. We are made as we are made, and the only action that defines us is the action of God. He defined us when He first designed us at the beginning. He acted again when He gave His Son as a replacement for each of us in death. As individuals, He acted to bring each of us into the world, His pleasure unparalleled in what He has made in each and every person. He is the proudest of the proud parents, and no failure (or perceived failure) of ours changes that.

The only thing that keeps us from the love of God is being separated from Him, and the thing that most separates us from Him is being someone we are not. His love for us does not change when we come with an outward appearance that does not reflect the inner creation. What we craft to represent us simply serves to block the reception of true love. The image we put on outwardly cannot receive the blessing of the authentic individual. Let me give an example.

Jacob ("deceiver") came in the outward appearance of his brother Esau and received the blessing of his father, Isaac. Jacob dressed himself in the manner of his brother and stole what was meant for his older brother. You may say, yes, but Jacob was blessed because of that. Jacob was blessed because the blessing was pronounced, and because it was always God's intention to bless him, but he was given to as someone other than himself. He lived his life in the blessing knowing always that what he had was intended for another. He lived under the shame of knowing that he cheated his brother. He lived with a fear that kept him from returning to his home. He lost so many blessings—family, love, peace, the trust of his brother and father—all because he stole what was not meant for him (Gen. 27).

It was over fourteen years before he came face to face with God and his identity was redeemed. He was finally given a new name and received the blessing he was chosen to receive by God's ordination (Gen. 32). It was always planned that he receive the blessing his father gave him, but it was through a lie that he usurped the place of his brother. It took all those years for him to come full circle and live in the fullness of what was planned for him. He took through the flesh (the outer man) what was meant for him all along in his spirit (the inner man). Religion defeats us because it is based on our own ability to bring forth God's will, and we are inherently unable to do so by design. God's will is best released through us by the presence of His life within us, and He only dwells in relationship because that is His very being: Father, Son, and Holy Spirit in One.

Another good example is the story of Jehu's appointment to the throne of Israel. Elisha the prophet sends one of the company of prophets to Jehu to anoint him king, and tells the messenger that after he anoints Jehu, to "open the door and run; don't delay" (2 Kings 9:20)! Elisha is telling him to get his job done and run away because Jehu acts like a madman. After Jehu becomes king, he moves to cleanse Israel of the sins of Ahab and Jezebel's reign. He goes after Joram, king of Judah (Ahab and Jezebel's son) and shoots him in the back with an arrow while Joram is running away.

After Joram is lying dead, killed by Jehu's arrow, "Jehu said to Bidkar, his chariot officer, 'Pick him up and throw him onto that field that belonged to Naboth the Jezreelite. Remember how you and I were riding together in chariots behind Ahab his father when the Lord made this prophecy about him: 'Yesterday I saw the blood of Naboth and the blood of his sons, declares the Lord, and I will surely make you pay for it on this plot of ground, declares the Lord.' Now then, pick him up and throw him on that plot, *in accordance with the word of the Lord*'" (2 Kings 9:25–26, Italics added). The new king wants to make sure that his actions are in keeping with the Word of the Lord.

Here was a man whose religious zeal for the Lord served the purpose of God to cleanse Israel of wickedness during a time of great departure from the Lord. However, I have to wonder how in line with God he was in his actions. When you have to make your behavior line up with God's word by moving the body of a man you have killed to another location, it makes me wonder what you traded up for. In this instance, one kind of self-determination is replaced by another. Ahab's idolatry, murder, and self-indulgent rule over Israel looked worse, but did Jehu's reckless passion really yield a better result for himself or the nation?

In the end, it says this of Jehu: "Yet Jehu was not careful to keep the law of the Lord, the God of Israel, *with all his heart*...In those days the Lord began to reduce the size of Israel. Hazael overpowered the Israelites throughout their territory east of the Jordan in all the land of Gilead..." (2 Kings 10:31–33, Italics added). Jehu acted out of his own religious mind, and ultimately did not keep the word of the Lord in his heart. He manipulated the word of the Lord to suit his actions. He was blessed in part because of his actions (2 Kings 10:30), but in the end his heart was not pure toward the Lord and the result diminished the blessing on his own life, and on those around him, namely Israel.

In the same way we are diminished by religion. That is what it really comes down to. It is not that God will not bless us. We may not even miss out on our calling. What we will get is less than we were meant to have, and we might even cause the people around us to be diminished by our selfish actions. God is looking for us not only to renew the relationship He planned for us, but to walk with Him in restoring the people in our lives and the church to the fullness of relationship with Him. Those relationships really require all of us to be fully ourselves, reaching out to one another in love to exhort and encourage a love and a life greater than we could ever achieve on our own. Religion will keep us from that life. Jesus has set us free to live as one—one whole individual and one whole church.

Chapter 3

CREATED FOR LOVE

A LIFE LIVED WITH GOD CANNOT BE summed up easily. It cannot be put into a container or explained in simple terms. I can say many things about Him, and a lot about my personal ways of interacting with Him. I can say a great deal about good theology, or explain in sound teaching concepts of the Law and grace. I can expound on the reality of miracles and speaking in tongues and God's power to transform lives. I can do all of that and you would still not understand.

Explaining a relationship is something more like explaining a river, or a mountain, or the movements of the wind. It is far more simple and extravagant than any of us will really understand. We can go swimming, but it doesn't mean we understand a river. We can go sailing but it doesn't mean we know the wind. We can climb a mountain but it doesn't mean that we can penetrate its depths.

God is a person that we cannot physically touch, but when He touches us, it is beyond words. When He touches my heart, it has moved me to tears, causing me to come face to face with pain that I needed to let go.

He has caused me to tremble. He has brought me to my knees. He has helped me to grieve. He causes me to laugh and sing. He is my best friend and the one Person I trust more than anyone I have ever known. God loves me more than anyone ever could and understands me in ways that no one has ever tried. He made me, and so He knows me more intimately than I even know myself.

God has gripped my heart and my mind and changed me. He has changed me because He wanted to set me free from the lies that had come to define me with confusion and fear and hatred. He did not change me because I was a disappointment to Him as I was, but because He wanted me to have so much more than I would have planned or expected for my own life. He has a more wonderful plan for me than I could ever have, more than I could imagine, and still He engages my imagination so that I can grasp what He has in mind. He causes me to move because I want to come to Him. He causes me to love because I see Him loving others.

This Love creates transformation unlike any other love. When we love and we give away love, we never remain the same. We become different. We are affected by the experience. We are softening ourselves for the sake of another. We are risking ourselves for someone else. When we love God, we are loving pure Love. To love God and others at the risk of ourselves is to be like Jesus, and in drawing close to Him, we will be changed. When we invite Him in, we welcome absolute relationship. When we open ourselves to Him, we are cleansed because He is stronger than a river, we are moved because He is more powerful than the wind, and we are lifted because He is higher than a mountain. All of this might seem very basic and unimpressive to say, but if you let Him reveal Himself to you, it becomes clear that He is more than expression can allow.

If you are willing to let God come into your life, into your heart, into your mind, He will show you what it is to be with Him. He is the only one who can do it. You cannot understand God by your effort. You can only understand God because He shows Himself to you. It is only up to us to let go of what we expect and what we need to see, and wait to see what He will reveal. It can be very scary in and of itself. It has been overwhelming for me many times in my life. Many times I have wanted to give up on God. Many times I have screamed and yelled and cursed at God. I have smashed walls, kicked doors, broken plates on the floor, and just flat out shaken my fist in the air. I have told Him that I would kill Him if He had the guts to come in person.

I have had a lot of repenting to do for my outbursts against God, and I do not share my behavior as an example to follow, but to say that it was honest coming from me. My broken heart and life opened on God like molten lava when He began to touch the deepest and most painful parts of me. I vomited hatred on Him. He just held me. That is who He is. That is the person who wants to listen to you, talk to you, and take you into Himself to love you. The reality of my death threats to God is that He did come in person, and the really painful truth is that I did kill Him. He chose death on the cross because I held my hatred against Him, and He refused to hold it against me. Seeing that changed me. He was able to make that real to my heart because I was real with Him.

I am more alive today because I was honest with God and in the midst of my foolishness, He came and restored me and reassured me that I am His. It is through our transparency about who we are now that God can work to show us who we were made to be. God can live through anyone who is willing to confess their present reality, accept the need to repent (which literally means to change your mind), and receive His reality.

Some of my walk with God has been so excruciating that I would have rather died outright. I have told Him as much. Yet I am still here. Fortunately, He didn't listen to me on those occasions. I mean, He heard me, but He decided I was wrong. Everything that He has brought me through, and asked me to face in myself and in others, has all been for a life that is greater than I could have ever expected. It is not because I am financially set for life or because I have the best car in the parking lot at work, or because I never have a bad day. It is not for any reason that makes real sense from a practical standpoint. It is all because having seen Him, I could not imagine living without ever seeing Him again.

Seeing Him face to face is what my every day is about. Not just in heaven one day many years from now, but seeing God face to face as often as I can. Seeing Him every day and longing more and more to see Him and hear Him and be touched by the God that I cannot put my hands on right now, but will be able to one day. He is more real to me than anything I can put my fingers around. He is amazing beyond description, and you can only discover that by letting Him come and show you.

Perhaps what I really want to say here is that God is safe for you to be yourself with under any condition. He is not waiting to pounce when you get it wrong, or even when you act flat-out horrific. He isn't even looking to tell you how bad your behavior is (most of the time). What He really wants you to understand is that it's all supposed to be better than this. It's not that *we* are supposed to be "better," but that life was intended to be incredible—and that is not about what you have or don't have. It's about a life beyond the one we typically even see. It is a life more full of, well, life. It is what Jesus called the abundant life. It is full of living. It is about enjoying everything more.

It might sound silly, but it's like when you first fall in love—except it never goes away. Food tastes better, flowers are more beautiful, you find yourself singing when you walk around, and you want to dance and do ridiculous things. Love makes you act out of the ordinary, and loving God makes you act straight from the supernatural. It is completely human, but more than we could be on our own. That is what we are made for.

We are not created to spend our lives breaking. That is why we break so badly. We weren't made to break. It is not in our makeup. We were not made to be abused, hated, and disrespected. We were made for love—created to be loved and to love. We were not made to hate. It is unnatural to us in every way. We were not made to be beaten. We were not made for drunkenness. Why does the body reject these behaviors? When we are beaten, we bleed and bruise. When we get drunk, we get sick. The order of creation working in us naturally rejects these activities.

We were not made to handle sin, disease, and death. The body breaks down and fails under the strain of these unnatural effects. What we need to understand is that the deeper places in us are damaged by sin. It affects not only the body, but the soul and spirit. Death actually begins in the spirit of a person and reaches outward to the body over time. The body is simply the outward reflection of the inner person, and God has come to love you back to wholeness.

Chapter 4

IN THE IMAGE AND LIKENESS

ONE OF THE MOST IMPORTANT CONCEPTS in understanding the renewal of our identity is to grasp that we have been created in the image and likeness of God (Gen. 1:26). According to *Strong's Exhaustive Concordance of the Bible*, the Hebrew root word that is read as "image" can literally be translated as a "shade or phantom", and the root that is "likeness" can also mean "resemblance." I believe the Lord says this both ways because there is a distinctive difference. To say that we are the shade is almost to say that we are God's shadow, or more completely that we resemble (likeness) God's shadow (image). I love this illustration because when we stand in the sun and our shadow is cast, there is never a point at which our shadow is not connected to us. A shadow is completely dependent on the object creating the shade, just as we are created completely dependent on God. So let's continue to discuss how we are created in God's image.

It is important to understand that just as God is a three-part being in one whole, we are created as a three-part being. We have been created to resemble Him. God reveals Himself as Father, Son and Holy Spirit (Matt. 28:19). We are created with a spirit, a soul, and a body (1 Thess. 5:23). Jesus makes it extremely clear that there is plan for us to engage in relationship with the fullness of who God is. Jesus tells His disciples, "If anyone loves me, he will obey my teaching. My Father will love him, and we will come to him and make our home with him...But the Counselor, the Holy Spirit, whom the Father will send in my name, will teach you all things and will remind you of everything I have said to you" (John 14:23,26). God is fully expressed in relationship with Himself: Father, Son and Holy Spirit. We are to have relationship with God the Father, God the Son, and God the Holy Spirit.

You know, the Father is saying, "If you want to know me, you need to know my Son"; the Son is saying, "If you want to know me, you have to know my Spirit"; the Holy Spirit is saying, "If you want to know me, you have to know the truth, and Jesus is the true path to the Father." The Father doesn't talk about himself; He talks about the Son and Spirit. The Son doesn't talk about Himself; He talks about the Father and the Spirit. And the Spirit doesn't talk about Himself; He talks about the Son and the Father. The heart of God is completely selfless even unto Himself. He is fully surrendered and at peace with Himself because He is never prideful about who He is. There is absolute security in His being and His desire is to dwell in us. He brings His being into our being. If we are not fully surrendered in our being—spirit, soul, and body—we will lack the full connection to His being that we were created for because we will lack the fullness of relationship we were created for. We were made in His image and the only way we come into fullness is to surrender to being remade through a relationship with the One we resemble.

God continues to reflect the nature of His Being and ours in the construction of the tabernacle. The design for the tabernacle was conveyed from God to Moses as having three distinct and separate areas, but all were held within one overall perimeter, just as our visible body contains all the aspects of our being. The tabernacle consisted of the outer court, the inner court, and the Holy of Holies. As with God, each aspect of our being has a different purpose and role to play in the way we relate to ourselves and in our relationships to others.

The outer court was a courtyard that anyone could access, just like anyone who is looking can see our physical body. In the tabernacle, the outer court is also where sacrifice took place, to gain the remission of sin. The apostle Paul speaks of "the law of sin at work within me," rhetorically asking the question, "Who will rescue me from this body that is subject to death" (Rom. 7:23–24)? This shows sin as working in what would be the outer court of a person—the body—where mortal death takes place. It is no coincidence that Jesus made the final and complete sacrifice for the remission of sin by His bodily death. Therefore, we see that Jesus is the aspect of God that represents the body.

The soul would then parallel the Holy Place, and the spirit the Most Holy Place. I want to say at this point that these are Biblical illustrations that help us to understand the mysterious nature of God, and they are designed to point us to relationship with God. This is not science and these are not absolute parallels. What I really want us to take away from this is that the inner being, that part of us which is unseen, is the place of surrender to God and all that He has to offer.

We are the tabernacle of God and we are to build a place of worship through our lives. It is through our inner being that true worship occurs. "Yet a time is coming and has now come when the true worshippers will worship the Father in the Spirit and in truth, for they are the kind of worshipers the Father seeks. God is spirit, and his worshipers must worship in Spirit and in truth" (John 4:23–24). It is from the innermost place of our spirit that we must worship God. Part of the whole of worship is praise, but the greater part of worship is in lifestyle.

"Therefore, I urge you, brothers and sisters, in view of God's mercy, to offer your bodies as a living sacrifice, holy and pleasing to God—this is your true and proper worship"(Rom. 12:1). God longs for each of us to offer our bodies as a sacrifice of worship to Him because it is recognition of the body as the dwelling of God, and sur-rendering it to Him as His own is the purpose of God. The fullness of beauty in God's plan is having Him living within us to connect in constant relationship. This is not an instant gratification relationship, but it is a life-giving flow that gives Him the place to move through us without interruption. The life we were intended to have is one without disconnect, without any hint of separa-tion; it is a life that overflows in every way through us and outward to others. When we open the tent of our life to be the tabernacle of God, it is an invitation for God to restore His original intention and have His presence rest on our hearts forever, just as His presence once rested over the tabernacle. "Now the one who has fashioned us for this very purpose is God, who has given us the Spirit as a deposit, guaranteeing what is to come" (2 Cor. 5:5).

So then, God enters into communion with us through His Spirit, passing into our spirit, soul, and body. This is an ongoing process that continually brings life into us. That ongoing flow of life was the plan, is the plan, and always will be the plan. This is the life of God, which He wanted for us from the foundation of the earth. It is the relationship we were made for. Every aspect of our being and behavior is designed to be directed by God's Spirit speaking to our inner being so we can choose God's plan and allow our connection with Him to be the motivation of our lives.

Just as the tabernacle was created not only for personal reconciliation but also for the whole community of God's people, His plan for unity continues in our relationship to God's body, the church. We are exhorted to "make every effort to keep the unity of the Spirit through the bond of peace. There is one body and one Spirit, just as you were called to one hope when you were called— one Lord, one faith, one baptism; one God and Father of all, who is over all and through all and in all" (Eph. 4:3–6). It is not an accident that God is mentioned in this passage as Father, Son [Lord], and Spirit. How do we make every effort to keep the unity "of the Spirit"? We need to remember that we are connected not only with one another, but with every aspect of God's being. If we are to see the church fully expressed according to God's intentions it will require every person to individually surrender to the fullness of God, and to remain mindful of the truth that we are called together into His being, not into a building. Coming into the fullness of our identity is not only for us as individuals, but it will redefine the identity of the church as we know it.

Chapter 5

THE INNER PLACE

A S WITH ANY EARTHLY RELATIONSHIP, the only way to experience God is to spend time with Him. To bring His life into ours we must include Him in as much of our lives as we can. This takes time and does not have to be done by force. Let it happen naturally. If we let the life of God begin to flow through our lives it will become an easy part of living. We should invite Him to be with us in the things we do and ask Him what He thinks about things. We should ask Him about the things He is doing, and let Him show us things. We should talk and interact with Him in everything we do.

Let what is coming into your heart come to the surface. This will do two things: first, it will allow God to bring areas of your life that need to be cleansed into view so that you can speak with Him about removing them. That is important. Let God remove the things that need to be removed and replace them with what needs to take the place of that thing. It is very important that whenever something is removed, God comes in and takes the place of the old thing. A clean spot needs a new resident—God is that resident. You want God occupying every place within you.

The second development that will occur by allowing what is in your heart to motivate your relationship with God is the realization that He has written His desires within you, and they will become more and more your own thinking, feeling, and believing. "Now what I am commanding you today is not too difficult for you or beyond your reach. It is not up in heaven, so that you have to ask, 'Who will ascend into heaven to get it and proclaim it to us so we may obey it?' Nor is it beyond the sea, so that you have to ask, 'Who will cross the sea to get it and proclaim it to us so we may obey it?' No, the word is very near you; it is in your mouth and in your heart so you may obey it" (Duet. 30: 11–14). God puts in our hearts His desires so that we can walk with Him in those desires. He makes what is unnatural in our sinful state, natural in our reborn state.

His desire is that we come to enjoy the time we spend with Him, the life we have through Him, and the place He has in us. We were made to enjoy God, just as He enjoys us, and it is His desire to cause that enjoyment to explode in us, overcome us, and set us free to live a life of beauty, majesty, and joy. He wants us to have His life in us, which is Him in us. And there is nothing more pleasurable than Him in the entire world. He is the greatest joy, the greatest love, ever. He is more than we can anticipate, more than we can imagine, more than we could plan for, more than we want, but not more than we need. We need Him in every way.

It is a great wonder and amazing thing that God created us for love. He made us for joy. He planned that we would have beauty and wonder and delight as part of our everyday lives. What we have had without Him is such a cheap imitation; it cannot be explained how much more there is available to our lives with Him.

We can choose to let Him in and make a place for Him to dwell in us. We can do this by reading the Bible, singing worship songs, and speaking prayers of all kinds, but we do it best by listening to His voice. Again, the ability to hear the voice of a person we cannot hear with physical ears takes time to develop; we can learn to hear God in our innermost being, just as we can allow Him to live in that place. Likewise, we can learn to know when what is coming out of our hearts was put there by Him. He has made us to hear Him, to connect with Him, and that is what we need to do again. We need to have Him in our moment-to-moment lives as much as possible, learning Him more and more each day. We need to involve Him in everything we do, to listen to Him in every choice we make, and to ask and wait for Him when we are unsure.

He will not abandon us to our own devices, but we have to choose to grow in this relationship just like any other relationship. If we invest in the lives of a spouse or a child, doesn't it make sense that we need to invest in God? It is what we were made for, and so will benefit every part of our own person as well as every relationship we have. He wants us to create connections with everyone around us so that life flows from Him, through us, and overflows to others.

We have to remember that good disciplines are important, but this is a love relationship and not a life of study and religious exercises. We read the Bible so we can develop ears for God's voice and understand the nature of His words—His gracious truth and kind severity. We pray for others and ourselves so we can touch God's heart and get in tune with Him. We worship because we have fellowship with an awesome God, and He is worth our praise and the attention we give in celebrating Him.

What we cannot do is make the works of our faith out to be an end in themselves. These are opportunities to enter into deep experiences with God. We need to connect with God, we need to be touched by Him deep within, we need to know that we have been kissed and held by a God whose hands we cannot see. We should remember the scars that are still cut into His hands and feet and head for us, and so remember, all the more, that we are called to share in His suffering so that we can also share in his glory (Rom. 8:17). This is perhaps one of the most difficult aspects of fellowship with God, but one that cannot go overlooked.

Chapter 6

SHARING IN GLORY

SOMETIMES WE EXPERIENCE GOD THROUGH the suffering we endure. So long as we remain on the earth, we will have to grapple with the harsh realities of pain and suffering. This is not only true of those who walk with God, but all people. In some way, we all lack, are all weak, are all in need; at the very least, we will be touched by the destructive behavior of some we come in contact with. Some of us will face pain and suffering from those who should be the closest to us. Others will face the ongoing societal injustices that plague our world due to the fallen decisions of our leaders, communities, and countries. The whole creation cries out for deliverance from the destruction of sin, pain, and death that surrounds us daily (Rom. 8:18–23). The suffering we face is another opportunity to turn our eyes to our Maker and Love, Jesus, and gain insight through the eyes of the Person who truly understands suffering.

One thing I really want to make clear about suffering and difficult times is that we should never expect suffering as a lifestyle or that everything we have in Jesus comes with suffering and pain. I have known many people, including myself, who have seen God this way, and it is such a destructive lie. Suffering is a frequently covered theme in Scripture because it so common, but it is talked about so that we have a means of walking through life's most painful experiences side-by-side with God, who is our Comforter and Counselor. Suffering is an aspect of life that we will participate in while we are here on the earth, but it is not a lifestyle. Suffering is passing away, just as much as death, disease, pain, and everything else that has come into the world as a result of sin. Suffering is a result of sin, whether it is our own sin and we are facing the consequences of our misalignment with God, or whether it comes because of the sins of others.

When I think of suffering, I think of the excruciating pain of the cross. The word *excruciating* was actually invented to describe the pain of crucifixion because a word did not yet exist to describe the horrifying pain of that form of torture. Jesus knows a thing or two-thousand about pain and suffering, and He is still the most joyful and loving person you can ever know. Hebrews 12:2 encourages us to remember Jesus: "for the joy set before him he endured the cross, scorning its shame, and sat down at the right hand of the throne of God." If we choose to walk through our suffering with Jesus, we have the chance to gain new understanding about love, forgiveness, and relationship.

God is consistently revealing the suffering and blood of Jesus so that He can reveal the life of God that we were created for. The suffering is always revealed for a moment so that we can be raised into life forever. The resurrection is the real key to life and power. Every time we come into a difficult situation, every time we are betrayed, every time we have to deal with hatred, rejection, and scorn, we have the choice to go to the cross where we both humble ourselves and release others from judgment as Jesus did for us at the cross. Once that is accomplished, we have the chance to enter the resurrection. Every time we suffer and rise again, we experience the resurrection. The apostle Paul made this powerful statement of faith that I love: "I want to know Christ—yes, to know the power of his resurrection and participation in his sufferings, becoming like him in his death, and so, somehow, attaining to the resurrection from the dead" (Phil. 3:10–11). What is Paul's focus here? He wants to know Jesus. He understands that the true value of suffering is relationship. To become like Jesus in His death is to enter into forgiveness when others have done nothing to warrant our forgiveness.

Suffering is the opportunity to press into the heart of God. It is our opportunity to see the truth about those who are hurting us, as well as to seek understanding about God's purpose, for our good, in allowing us to walk through the situations that grind against us. When we seek God in those times, we open ourselves up to His speaking. We open up to the power of Life in us and that will cause us to rise to any challenge. Resurrection power is the power to enter into the reality of heaven and bring heaven into an earthly situation. This is the will of God: His kingdom coming on earth as it is in heaven. That is the resurrection. That is moving in the Spirit of life rather than accepting the present situation as an eternal truth.

Resurrection is the choice we have as children of God. "Now if we are children, then we are heirs—heirs of God and co-heirs with Christ, *if indeed we share in his sufferings* in order that we may also share in his glory" (Rom. 8:17, italics added). That is the power within us for love, for joy, for peace, for goodness, kindness, gentleness, temperance, and patience. That is bearing fruit in keeping with repentance. That is life, and that is the fire of God removing everything that death has convinced us will last forever.

Chapter 7

ALL CONSUMING FIRE

I N A VERY PRACTICAL WAY, FIRE IS A FAN-
tastic cleanser. Precious metals are a great example
of this. We use fire to remove the impurities from
treasures found in the earth. It's almost like God pur-
posed a natural illustration to speak to us by putting
precious metals deep into the dirt of the earth so that
one day we would find them, melt them down to purify
them, and attribute value to them for their beauty and
rarity. I'm not much for coincidence when it comes to
God planning ahead. I do not think it is an accident that
we were formed from dirt (Gen. 2:7), God calls Himself a
consuming fire (Deut. 4:24), and that we hold treasure in
jars of clay (2 Cor. 4:7).

As a new believer trying to understand relationship
with God, He gave me a verse from the Psalms to understand the work of His fire within us: "And the words of
the LORD are flawless, like silver refined in a furnace of
clay, purified seven times" (Ps. 12:6). Just as God's nature
is love, He is a consuming fire, and when He makes us
His dwelling, we have a fire living in us that will consume
everything. Just as silver mined from the earth will have
all impurities removed from it when it is heated by fire,

so will our lives when Jesus comes to live in us. That is what it looks like for God to live in us because the fire is violent, and the fire is loving. He puts His words in us through Jesus, and purifies us until nothing in us diminishes the treasure of Jesus in us. This process continues "seven times," which is the Biblical number for eternity. God continues to purify us until nothing remains but the eternal nature that Jesus bestows on our authentic being. When Jesus comes, He brings the baptism of the Holy Spirit and fire (Matt. 3:11).

The baptism of water is for repentance from sin as we place our faith in Jesus for our salvation. The baptism of fire is for the process of removing everything that diminishes our true nature. We receive salvation by faith, and it is at that moment we are given the chance to enter into a lifestyle only revealed through fire. When the Holy Spirit comes into your life, He comes with a fire that wants to consume every part of you. He comes to take possession of your being, to love with passion, and to remove everything that gets between you and Him.

As a new believer, I was overflowing with zeal. I was passionate, willing, and ready to preach Jesus everywhere I went. Zeal for his house consumed me (Ps. 69:9; John 2:17). For me this was like the passion of a teenage love. I was excited and emotional but lacking in wisdom, and "…it is not good to have zeal without knowledge, nor to be hasty and miss the way" (Prov. 19:2). But this zeal was a fire in me. In my zeal, I pursued God through Scripture knowledge. This knowledge became a place from which I could show others what was right and what was wrong— Jesus is right and everything else is wrong. That was the line I was pushing, but it was all coming from the wrong spirit. It was a "ye know not what manner of spirit ye are of" (Luke 9:55, KJV), "call down fire from heaven" spirit instead of the Holy Spirit. I had a hard edge based on my knowledge of good and evil instead of the flow of life. The passion and excitement burned in me and moved me, and the moving made me look for God. In passionately seeking God, I was burned in the fire of God's love and mercy, and in being burned, I was refined. God revealed Himself in deeper and deeper places within me so that I would choose to move more completely into His life.

The knowledge of Scripture that is life giving is the growth of a heart and mind from which you can test and discern the voice of God. In this way, we can listen and move with Him, moment to moment, as He reveals His timely and loving will for each situation. This is in stark contrast to having a lot of scriptural head knowledge that becomes a library of information from which you choose what is right and wrong in a given moment or situation. One way is based on God's direction and life, and the other is based on our direction and leads to death, because the Spirit gives life, but the letter kills (2 Cor. 3:6).

Another way that I have experienced God's fire is by seeing Him face to face. In Revelation 1:14, it says of Jesus that His eyes are like fire. Over the years, He has looked at me with those eyes of fire. This has not been every time He shows Himself to me, but often when He really needs to send something straight into my heart. He looks at me with those eyes of fire to soften the hard places and move more directly into my inner being. He has done this many times because He has so often had to overcome my internal resistance to His love. Although I knew the truth of His love in my head, it was not in my heart. I had not believed His love was for me. I was only seeing love as fuel for my religious zeal rather than the open hand and heart of a lover.

Jesus is not longing to develop an army of religious fanatics, but rather to bring to life a family of passionate lovers. We are called for the sole purpose of loving and living out of love. Everything in our lives is meant to flow from the exchange of love between Jesus and us. What is more passionate and intimate? What will change you faster than seeing the fire of God burning in the eyes of Jesus, who is saying, "I love you"? Just breathe that in for a moment. Eyes of fire, Jesus face to face, I love you, I love you, I love you—you are a masterpiece of beauty and I love you! That is Jesus. That is the Lover. That is the fire of being face to face with Jesus.

Just as much as He is looking for our hearts through His eyes of fire, He is longing for us to look for His heart, to see into the fire of His eyes and listen to the heart in Him. He longs to be loved just as we do. If we are longing to be loved, and we all are, He is longing with all the intensity of eternal longing, unending passion, and unfailing love to have His love return to Him through us. We are worth all that to Him and more than I can convey, or we could imagine. If every person in the world who has touched the heart of God, experienced His love, were to get together and imagine as one person the love and passion of God, our description wouldn't come close to the fullness of His being. He is unsearchable, but altogether wonderful, amazing, and lovely in every way. That is Jesus.

God's continual presence within us catches us on fire and everything that we have made by our own effort is burned up so that true life can replace the limited lives we make. God wants to consume our limitations, all our self-made efforts, and release His glory through us. He wants to restore us to the outworking of His efforts. He wants to give us the life that He intended. The key to this is releasing the life that we have planned and made for ourselves. We have to choose to surrender our efforts and allow God to give us the wisdom and insight to join with His efforts.

We can choose to partner with God in His life, but our plan cannot live in the same space as God's plan. What we have thought was good and what God is revealing will conflict. Even in following God openly and willingly, I have mostly found that the outcome I expected was not what God had planned. I still think too small and with too many limitations. He is without limit. That limitless life is what He wants to give us, to share with us, to experience with us. He wants to be with us in it—more accurately, He wants us to be with Him in it.

When He comes in fire, it is a connection with God, through the Holy Spirit, that is designed to bring violence to the kingdom of self that we have created and ruled over. God is the only acceptable King over our lives. In the most basic terms, He is looking to conquer our selfish little kingdom and establish His own place as Lord. He does not want to rule because He is a heavy-handed, controlling dictator, but He wants to rule so He can restore us to the kingdom of heaven, which is filled with peace, life, love, and plenty of everything beautiful, kind, and good.

He wants to remove the broken pieces of life that we have tried to fashion into a covering, as Adam and Eve once did long ago with some fig leaves. In realizing that we are naked, without a proper covering, we try to cover ourselves with whatever is available even if it is completely deficient. God wants to cover us with His Being, which was our initial garment. We were once covered by His presence. His glory, which is His fiery presence in us mingling with the true nature of our created beings, is what restoration through Jesus brings us. Holy Spirit comes with the glory of God and touches us with His presence where nothing that is separate from Him can live. So when we come into His presence, everything that is dead is burned up, like silver being purified to reveal a product of great worth.

The relationship with Jesus that is exposed by His fire moving through us is the most valuable treasure we can possibly gain because it is life from the dead. The more life we have in us, the more we can live in His presence, the more known by Him we become, the more like Him we become, and the more love we receive and can give. Who doesn't want more love? It's not that He loves us more; He simply removes the limitations to experience so we can taste the love that is always available in Him. The fire unlocks the truest desire of God for all His people: that we live and breathe in the ongoing presence and experience of Love.

Chapter 8

BECOMING YOU

G OD MADE YOU. HAVE YOU GOTTEN that so far? If you can accept that, then we can explore the next level: God made you to be you. He created you to be the way He made you to be. He did not make you to be the way that others expect you to be, to act according to their demands or desires, to carve yourself up into little pieces trying to please the world. He made you to be you, and as much as Jesus wasn't liked by everyone around Him, we will not be either.

No matter how hard we try, we will be rejected by others. It's true. It's in the Bible. Haven't you experienced this? It's not how God designed it to be, but it is something that we have to face in this broken world if we are to live the life we were made to live. You might be the most special, amazing, beautiful person on the planet, but someone will find a bone to pick with you. Maybe numerous *someones*. The truth is we are all special, amazing, and beautiful, and the only person who might have a harder time accepting that than those around us, is us.

How many of you reading, when I wrote you are special, amazing, and beautiful, had an internal response

41

that rejected that statement? Was your hidden (or not so hidden) response saying, "Oh, of course!" or "No, not me"? I would say that both of those reactions are rejecting the truth of how glorious you are. They are the chosen cover up. Really knowing who you are doesn't require a response. Knowing just is. It is as much an immovable truth as grass being green or the sky being blue. We might not understand fully why it is so, but we know beyond question and beyond defense that it is.

When you know who you are, it is unwavering, and it is because God told you who you are. It is because your inner being heard the voice of God and you were willing to take the risk to agree that God is right. I say risk that God is right because it is so easy for us to reject the truth of who God says we are. Our frightened minds, which have been often lied to, are too quick to say, "I know," or "No, not me." Knowing who you are begins by accepting who God is. It comes by both believing in Him and by accepting His voice—accepting the words the Holy Spirit speaks into your inner being, accepting the touch of His hand, accepting that He does speak and touch and move.

I have to say that if we want to know who we are, we have to know who God is and trust that He knows us better than we know ourselves. We are, as we have discussed, made in His image and likeness. Wouldn't it make sense that we are like Him? Doesn't it stand that there are things about Him that are reflected in us? When I talk about knowing God, I do not mean just having a quiet time, or getting into a Bible study, or hours of worship and intercession. I am not talking about spiritual training or exercise, or even disciplines. All of those aspects of engaging God are wonderful and necessary, but I am talking about opening yourself up to accept who He is. When I talk about knowing God, I mean letting Him be Himself with you.

When I first gave my life to God, I was twenty-two. I lay on my bedroom floor on an incredibly hot day in July and wrote out a prayer. I really didn't even have the capacity to pray at the time, so I wrote. I wrote that if He would bring joy into my life, remove my pain, help me to understand why I was alive and what I was made for, He could have my whole life. It is so hard for me to explain the extreme way in which He immediately answered me, has continued to answer me, and done more than I could have ever thought to ask for. What happened for me was a total transformation. God poured into me a hunger for the Word, and I ate. God gave me a desire to go to church, and I built relationships. God endowed me with a desire for prayer, and so I prayed. God moved my heart to witness to others about His love and how He touched my life, and so I spoke. The more I yield my life to what He has placed in me, the more I see Him, the more I see who I am made to be.

I think it is hard to explain because it is so personal and so intimate. Trying to describe intimacy with God is difficult in the way it is difficult to explain how beautiful it is to experience intimacy with your lover—and yet it is far more than that. It is difficult to explain the beauty of having your Maker breathe inside you and fill your being with life. It is powerful, and it will change you, but it is something you have to have for yourself. It really can't be given by someone else. It can be spoken of, but words will always fall short.

This lack of transference is why the Bible cannot change anyone without a real interaction with Jesus. You might read the Bible and follow its teaching, but unless reading becomes relationship, leading to transformation, you will probably only become some version of a "better" person. This is the ongoing problem with what we create apart from God. Can we really be "better" people or simply be completely ourselves? God is not interested in "better" people doing things their way. He delights in us as we are and wants to have a partnership that is full of life and love. How we change just by being in His presence is a matter of course. It is impossible to spend time with God and not be changed. "...We know that when Christ appears, we shall be like him, for we shall see him as he is" (1 John 3:2).

God is constantly expanding our view of Him. He is growing our ability to see Him, to see as He sees and be as He is in His love because all life comes through that love. Everything good that has been given has been a gift of His love. From the very creation of the earth for our good, to the creation of man as His partner, to the sacrifice of His Son to restore man to that place at His side, it has been because of His passion for us. He dreamt of having us with Him, did everything to put us there at first, and then to bring us back after we departed. He is unwavering in His willingness to exchange what we have made for what He made. It is His indescribable pleasure to give us everything. All we have to do is open up to Him first.

A good friend of mine shared a fantastic revelation with me about how we open up to God. Before He went to the cross, Jesus speaks of how in the end times many will come to Him and, He will say, "Depart from me. I never knew you." My friend pointed out to me that Jesus says *He* does not know *them*. It is not that they do not know Him, but that He does not know them. This is God saying that He will not know those people. This is the same God who knows everything about us:

> For You did form my inward parts; You did knit me together in my mother's womb. I will confess *and* praise You *for you are fearful and wonderful and* for the awful wonder of my birth! Wonderful are Your works, and that my inner self knows right well. My frame was not hidden from You when I was being formed in secret [and] intricately *and* curiously wrought [as if embroidered with various colors] in the depths of the earth [a region of darkness and mystery]. Your eyes saw my unformed substance, and in Your book all the days [of my life] were written before they ever took shape, when as yet there was none of them.
>
> —PSALM 139:13–16, AMP

How is it possible that the God who created us could not know us? I believe it is because we can choose to not be known to Him. God will come to anyone who is willing to have Him, and He will know each person who is willing just as much as we are willing to be known. If we want to let God know us a little, we will be known a little. If we want Him to know us completely, He will come and know every aspect of our being. To those who want to be completely known, He will unlock every door, come into every room, and live in everything that is us. He wants to more than anything else. He made us to be known. Only we can keep Him out.

God loves us so much that He will never come into a place He is not invited to be. He will stand at the door and knock, but we must open the door. We must at least yell from across the room, "I am tied up on the other side of the room! Please come in and get these ropes off of me." He wants so much to come in, sit down, and eat with us. He wants to have a meal with us, and that means fellowship, it means family, it means provision, it means satisfaction—it means everything a meal shared between two people means. It is life giving and intimate. He is not coming in for McDonald's. He is coming in for a *meal*. This is going to take a while.

Chapter 9

CHOOSING TO
BE KNOWN

A LLOWING OURSELVES TO BE KNOWN BY God all starts with a choice. He wants us to *want* to be known. He wants us to surrender to His love. This is uncommon to most people. I know it was for me. In my experience, prior to tasting the love of God, my understanding of love showed it to be determined, forceful, and rather impatient. It was passionate, but not particularly close or yielding.

When God came into my life, I had no problem with things like zeal, passion, sacrifice, and an unrelenting God who wanted every part of my life. I did have a hard time with a patient, gentle, merciful and tender Jesus who would stand beside me in my failure. I had no idea how to relate to a person who showed me how the pieces of my life go together. I couldn't relate to a person who would build within me, for me. I could not understand a God like that. He baffled me. For many years I wanted that side of God, but had very little experience that allowed me to accept that about Him. I didn't experience it because when He came to me with kindness or gentleness, it took me a very long time to accept that it was Him and take in the love that He was offering me. Sometimes I still get confused in my experience of Him, but every day that I let Him know me, changes me. I have been shown so much about who I am through seeing Him. That is the plan. Him knowing me, revealing me; me knowing Him, revealing Him. That is the passion and love of a relationship with Jesus. That is the motivation for the choice to let Him come inside. That is the reality of surrender.

When I turned my life over to Jesus, I became part of a church that God had amazing plans for. He spoke many times, very clearly and specifically, about His intentions for our group and His plan to use us to reveal His kingdom. We were so blessed in so many areas, and had so many gifted people who really had a passion for God, all fellowshipping together. Over eight years I watched as we kept God out. We didn't keep Him out entirely, but we were very selective about what we let Him lead and what we held to in a way that we were comfortable with. We mostly kept God to the known quantities of Christian living instead of knowing Him and being known by Him.

Some of the choices to keep God out were made by the leaders, and some were made by other members of the body. In the end, the result was devastating. God moved on and decided to take many people with Him. Our church family went from over three hundred to around twenty-five people. It was so heartbreaking to see it happen. God had one plan, and enough of us had another that He could not move forward with that group.

We did not choose to let Him come in and know us.

We did not choose to have Him lead us, to really love us, into the place that would reveal Him. We would not risk failure, or even looking like failures, to let Him do what would most show who He is, to reveal to us a "success" that was different in nature than our experiences were informing us was correct and appropriate. The unpredictable nature of a God who is both knowable, and yet deeper than imagining, showed us an unbeaten path that we would not walk down—much to my sorrow and to the sorrow of many.

What I am saying is that God can be kept from doing what He wants to do. He can be held back from moving in power and according to His intentions if we are unwilling to choose Him, to risk on Him, and let Him be completely who He is. Jesus revealed this truth when He visited His hometown during the time of His earthly ministry. The people of His town knew Him as a carpenter who had been raised by Mary and Joseph. Jesus was the kid from down the street, back in town, and proclaiming that He can heal the sick and raise the dead. "Coming to his hometown, he began teaching them in their synagogue, and they were amazed. 'Where did this man get this wisdom and these miraculous powers?' they asked. 'Isn't this the carpenter's son? Isn't his mother's name Mary, and aren't his brothers James, Joseph, Simon and Judas? And aren't all his sisters with us? Where then did this man get all these things?' And they took offense at him...And he did not do many miracles there because of their lack of faith" (Matt. 13:53–58). In the Gospel of Mark, it says "...he *could not* do any miracles there, except lay hands on a few sick people and heal them" (6:5, Italics added).

The Lord does not need us to do the things He desires to do, but He wants us to join Him in it. He wants it to be a step in building a relationship. He is happy to help anyone who desires help, but His passion is to lead people into a life fully connected to Him. That is the greatest help He can give. Sometimes we are allowed to suffer for a time so that we can gain a hunger to be filled in the place of our deepest need by Him.

When we do not risk our full surrender to be known by God, we risk the possibility that we might miss Him altogether. There is so much that will seek our attention in this world, with all its distractions, we need a deep understanding of our need, and it is all the more wonderful if our understanding becomes a passion for God that step by step falls more in love with Him. Really, even need can fall short in drawing us in if that is all the further we allow ourselves to go. We all need to be saved, we need to be loved, we need help and provision, but to come to God in absolute vulnerability does more than fill our need: it releases an unstoppable river of life.

If our invitation to God is as our "need-filler," we will expect a vending machine relationship where we give only to receive an expected quantity, but all we really get is junk food. Instead of running into the arms of a loving Father, we end up looking for a sugar daddy. God is no sugar daddy. He is altogether wonderful and passionately generous in His love, but His provision is for our good, not to meet our demands. He is not looking to raise a bunch of spoiled brats. He wants children who come looking for His love, move into His desires, and fall in love with His heart because in seeking, we find that He is truly the most beautiful person we have ever met.

Taking the steps to open ourselves up to Him, allowing Him to walk into us, is our choice. We have to come to lay it all down. We have to come to Him to let it all go. I have to say for me, even with my promise to God to do just that, it has been unbelievably difficult. It is a step-by-step process that happens one day at a time. He prepared us for this when He told us to take up our cross daily. And just when I think that I have laid it all down, He shows me one more area of thinking or acting that is a dead branch on the tree of my life. He always seems to find one more thing to prune out and remove from me. This is not because He is demanding and looking to tear my life apart to serve His own ends. He is really looking to make room in me so the life of His being can overflow from the place of residence. That is His purpose in everything. Our best is to be His home, as individual people and as one whole church—really one whole creation. This is all up to us. It is all a matter of how far we are willing to let Him come in. How deep are we willing to have Him penetrate? How much of our lives are we willing to let Him remodel and restore?

Chapter 10

THE COST OF FREEDOM

J UST AS THERE IS A COST TO REMAINING closed-off to God, true freedom will also cost you. The cost of being free is something many of us never really weigh, or simply do not think about. Many of us think that it is God's free gift and go about the business of being saved, thanking God that He took it all, but never get to the freedom part.

Now, first of all, it is important to say that God did pay the price—completely. There is nothing missing from what was paid for us. Freedom is not about the fullness of the debt being paid, but about settling the accounts within ourselves. We hold ourselves captives through the ledger we keep for ourselves, with God, and with those around us. We can develop accounts for un-forgiveness, guilt, shame, and judgements against others like we were storing up money for the future, but we are only storing up unsettled debts. The kingdom of God is a debt-free society. This is why scripture exhorts us to realize that love holds no account (1 Cor. 13:5, NAS).

The cost to us is in wiping our own ledger clean and letting our own kingdom crumble for the sake of His kingdom. It is Jesus who reminds us that only a fool begins building without thinking of the cost of finishing the work, "... for if he lays the foundation and is not able to finish it, everyone who sees it will ridicule him, saying 'This fellow began to build and was not able to finish'" (Luke 14:29–30).

It is so easy to forget that so much has been given to draw us close to God, and that for that payment, much is required. Still, in God's love, it is not a debt we owe, not a balance to be paid off, but a desire planted in our hearts by the Spirit that should grow into a love willing to give Him everything. We can never catch up to God's sacrifice by what we give, so the idea that we owe Him not only falls short, but is fallen in its very concept. Love simply gives without holding accounts.

I know for myself, over the years of walking with the Lord, I have had to weigh many times the price that it cost me to continue in His will, and all the while struggling to know His love for me. As I mentioned in the introduction, I have gone through a divorce. After nearly ten years of marriage, while in the midst of a second separation, I reached a point where I could no longer hold onto my marriage. As I had done many times before, I surrendered it to God. I sought His heart to refresh my heart with His love and compassion. So much of what I know about surrendering to relationship with God has come through the struggle of my former marriage because, despite all my efforts, all my surrender to my Beloved to know what it means to love someone as He does, my marriage never healed from the broken place it was at.

To be plain, it was a destructive relationship. There is

so much I could say about how my words and attitudes, especially in the early years, were cutting and full of anger. There is so much that could be said about the pain I carried through all those years from my behavior—the guilt and shame and self-hatred for all the pain I had caused. Nearly three years of marriage counseling with two different counselors left me in a place where the counselors and I really saw in me a man that was embracing transformation. I was able to accept the truth that my sin, my broken behaviors, my own pain from the past, had all been paid for. Forgiveness was mine, not by my effort to change, but by the love of my beautiful Jesus. It had taken quite a while for my behavior to really change because I wasn't able to reconcile the truth of who God was saying I am, His love for me no matter what, and the bombardment on my mind that nothing I was doing was bringing healing to the relationship. It was an impossible battle between the love of my Maker and my heart to love someone else in the way He does. To stand in the revelation that to be like Jesus is to enter the place of His sacrifice so as to win the heart of another. Despite all the new revelation, the healing from past wounds, the restoration of my identity, all of the new life in me did not translate into healing for the marriage. God, in His mercy, used every heart-breaking moment as a catalyst for my transformation. Although I would never want to experience anything so painful again, having passed through it, I wouldn't trade the depth of relationship with the Lord that emerged from that time.

I spent a great deal of time weighing out the cost of my marriage ending. I wondered what would happen if I stopped trying so hard to fix it, how it would affect the rest of my life if healing never came into the marriage, and what it would mean for my relationship with God. How could I continue in His love knowing that I had broken vows made, not only to Him, but to someone I had truly loved with all the depth I knew how? I did not want to give up, did not want to disappoint God. I just wanted to be a good son for my great Dad. But, I finally reached the point where I could not put one more foot in front of the other. I could not take one more breath in the air I was breathing. I could not face one more day of battle, trusting, hoping that it would all pan out in the end. I surrendered, trusting God that my heart was in His hands and that true restoration could only be found in Him.

Tremendously, the world did not collapse in the wake of my weakness. I did not die from God's wrath. After ten years of fighting and standing, fighting and standing, fighting and standing, everything I had sacrificed and fought for fell away. The moment I stopped fighting for it, my marriage passed away. And now, I have to wonder if it was just something that I was fighting for on my own. I used to tell people that every day was like waking up with wounds all over my soul, putting on the armor of God, knowing that I was bleeding to death underneath. My efforts came to end, and I laid before God crying out for help.

I suddenly realized perhaps the greatest truth that has ever broken through in my heart: I have limits. I came face to face with the reality that Joseph had grasped in prison, so that when he was asked to translate Pharaoh's dream, he responded, "I cannot do it...but God will..." (Gen. 41:16). I am not able, but God is. It seems like it should be so very basic, and perhaps the concept itself is, but through my experience with God I now own the knowledge. It has become part of me to know that my abilities to complete His works will never do. I will never be enough in my own strength and ability to complete the work of God in my life.

I had to give up to get it. I had to lose it all to really understand that I never had it to begin with. God has it, and He has me. I belong to Him, and so does everything I have, everything I can give away. The cost is like a father asking his son to bring bread to the neighbor who has a need. The father bought the bread, put it in the hands of his son, and sent him on his way to the neighbor.

There is no compulsion out of force, no pressure on our will to serve, to hunch like a slave that needs to grovel for his life, or his next meal. It is the nature of freedom that comes from God and flows through us to give freely. Once we are free, it is natural to show others how they might be free, and our freedom will give people cause to ask to be free. It is for freedom that Christ has set us free (Gal. 5:1). There is no other motive in Him but the simple desire that we be free. It becomes our desire to set others free because we become in tune with Him when we surrender our own desires to His.

Let me share a practical example of what it means to count the cost of freedom. I have been in construction my whole life. My dad is a carpenter, and I started at ten doing clean up on construction sites. I learned how to work hard and give my all every day. Twenty-five years later, I had become a construction manager, and part of my job was to write estimates for construction projects. I spent a good part of my week literally counting the cost for my boss. He would ask me to estimate the cost of building, and based on those calculations we would either get the job or not. Based on those prices we either made money or lost money. It required care and a great deal of knowledge about what is needed for building and how the construction process occurs.

In the estimating process, I rely first on the architect to give me an accurate set of blueprints from which I can read the design and discover the plan for construction. A good set of drawings will included individual sheets for the existing conditions, demolition, floor plans, electrical and plumbing layouts, heating and cooling specifications, details for interior finishing, elevations of the finished exterior and section drawings of the finished interior. They will include a vast array of notes and specifications. I also have to put a lot of trust in the contractors I will be working with on the project. My experience is in carpentry, and so my knowledge is mainly focused in that area. When I work on a quote I need to seek the expertise of an electrician, a plumber, HVAC contractor, tile installers, painters, excavators, and masons, just to name a few.

Eventually, if we get the job, it will be a group effort to complete the work. Once the work begins, every tradesman involved in the construction project is subject to, and needs to have knowledge of, the building codes for their area of expertise. These are the state and federal laws that dictate specific aspects of all phases of construction. These codes ensure that all the work is being done in a uniform and safe way, and they are designed to protect both the contractors and the owners of the building, not only for the present, but also for any future occupants. All of this knowledge and experience, laws and design, go into the creation or renovation of a building. And every aspect needs to be estimated prior to starting construction so the person paying for the project can determine if they can afford to do the work and have a quality home at the conclusion.

When we consider a life with God, we have to decide if we are going to restrict Him, or if we will partner in the work until His work is complete. He is the architect and has the perfect design that has been laid out for both the initial construction and renovation of our lives. He has included a lot of very specific instructions regarding every aspect of our design: how we are wired, what the finishes are supposed to look like, our purpose in being built according to His design. He uses those around us as subcontractors to help Him get the work done right. Like our building codes, He has His Word to protect both the worker and the homeowners. I liken it to a person, each unique in our creation, or to the church, as one building for God to dwell in.

If we understand the nature of our need for Jesus, and that we are all in need of renovation work in our lives (i.e. sanctification/healing/maturity) then we need to not only consider the cost, but also really apprehend the price of our relationship to God. We need to understand both the price that was paid, and the price that we must pay. What is God asking of us when He asks us to follow Him? What is the cost of the freedom that He offers? It is very difficult to estimate the cost when you do not understand what is being built. Many times over the years I have had to realize that what I thought God was doing was not what He was doing. Ultimately, this projected from two root issues: one, not really knowing God; two, projecting my desire onto God's plan and getting my sticky little fingers involved.

See, the tricky thing with building according to God's design is that we have very little reference point for who God is and what He is doing before agreeing to get involved with Him. We have no idea how much it will cost, and really have a limited way of understanding beforehand. I think the kingdom of God is like a man from France who wants to build a house in Russia and has no idea how to speak the language or what the conversion rate is from Euros to Rupees. We come to Jesus as foreigners looking for a home, and our fallen nature takes Him for a greasy real estate salesman.

We see a guy with this line about the greatest deal we will ever see, saying, "I have a great house for you. It's amazing. It's grand. You can't imagine it. It's yours without cost, but you have to sign the house you do own over to me. And oh, yeah, you can't see this new place before you sign on the dotted line." Now, if we have had any experience with Jesus, we might get some idea of what we are signing up for, but if He is still very much a person on a page, we're sitting there saying, "Whoa, buddy, wait a minute. I don't even know who you are. I would like to see this place before we sign the contract." And He smiles and says, "Trust me, you're gonna love it."

In the world we live in, that just screams, "*Scam*! Run for your life." But in His world, there is nothing more sincere and more real. He means it with every ounce of His heart, and He can deliver the goods. The choice we have is whether to buy in. Jesus' intention is to have us give to Him what we have created out of our vast limitation so He can give us what He has created from his vast unlimitedness. The final cost to us is exactly what it cost Him: a life fully surrendered to the will of the Father.

Chapter 11

THE NEED FOR FREEDOM

THE CHALLENGE WITH FREEDOM IS IDENTI-
fying it as different from captivity. Many times,
we get so comfortable with the prisons we make
for ourselves, or that other people have encouraged us
to accept, that we embrace inmate orange jumpsuits as
fashion forward and walking single file as the catwalk of
life. Our captivity becomes familiar, comfortable; therefore, it isn't seen for what it is. We are left living in an
illusion of freedom. However, captivity is easily identifiable. It is painful, fearful, lifeless, burdensome, has the
same scenery all the time, and it tends to be horribly
lonely. It may explode with anger, hatred, and jealousy. It
is hungry all the time, more in the soul than in the body,
but in the body also. Jesus will ask you to give all that up
to be truly free.

Freedom, on the other hand, is identifiable by its
marks of love, joy, peace, patience, kindness, goodness,
gentleness, faithfulness, and temperance. It is a place
of life that gives and receives relationship freely and
without limit. For most of us, this is more foreign than
the lives of abuse and destruction we typically accept as
"real life." The true life that Jesus promises is most often

viewed as impossible and inaccessible. And without our acceptance of Him, it is.

He will also ask you to give up all the ways that you try to imprison others. This is perhaps the greater challenge for some. My fears caused me to create many prisons for those around me. Of course, the choice to accept those prisons, to live in them, belongs to the people themselves, but my inner defenses were built on judgments, anger, bitterness, and self-righteousness. To my mind these devices made me strong, and it made others weak, and I believed that made me safe. In reality, it only made me lonely. My mental prisons did a lot to keep God and other people from loving me and very little to prevent me from getting hurt. It didn't make me stronger, it only made me tired.

Jesus tells us that in His house there are many rooms, and that He went to prepare a place for those that believe (John 14:2). In my house, there are many rooms also, and I had made places for people to fit according to my estimation of them. These rooms were designed to protect me by keeping the harmful actions of others away from me. I held people in my rooms so I could be safe, but very few of my relationships really had any life to them because the rooms were named for the weaknesses of others. In my mind, everyone was identified by his or her frailties and failures rather than the life that was in them. I did this without even thinking about it. Over many years of trying to protect myself, it just happened automatically.

In that way I believed I would not get hurt when others failed me in some way. All it really did was keep people away from me, stop me from seeing their love for me, hurt them because of my judgments, and break down the possibility of trust. My defenses never stopped me from getting hurt. They only stopped me from seeing the hurt I was causing others. It also stopped me from seeing the wonder in other people and the beauty of those around me.

As I have been set free from this mental pattern, having allowed God to get the demolition crew into the house of my mind and do some major renovations, my gift for seeing other people's broken places can be used according to God's intention—to help them get free. I can see the life, the beauty, the love that God has put in others more and more. In this sense, the cost of following Jesus is the destruction of what I have built on my own.

Psalm 127:1 says, "...Unless the Lord builds the house, the builders labor in vain..." What I had built was *my* house, and it was completely vain. It was based on my vanity, my pride, the notion that I could see all ends and make the right judgments about others. It was based on the idea that I could make a right judgment about myself. I assumed that I knew what I was supposed to be like. However, if I cannot clearly see who I am to be through my own eyes, how can I see others? The fallen nature of man is not only misinformed about itself but about others also. If we are truly going to build a house that pleases God, it is going to have to be a joint effort. We were not called to freedom alone, but as a whole body of Christ. "You, my brothers and sisters, were called to be free. But do not use your freedom to indulge the flesh;

rather, serve one another humbly in love" (Gal. 5:13). Our need for freedom is for all of us. We have been born again into God's family. The choice to live that life is ours.

The key to this freedom is allowing God to renew our minds. From the minute we are born, we are learning who we are through a fallen mind. Even with the noblest intentions, we are being taught who we are by other people who do not have all the right answers. By the time we are old enough to understand the idea of a personal identity, it is usually skewed by the knowledge we have had access to. When Jesus gets involved, the first step is removing the broken identity we have accepted about ourselves.

In "The Empire Strikes Back," Yoda tells Luke Skywalker that he must, "unlearn what he has learned." God takes it even further and tells us that we "...have been crucified with Christ and [we] no longer live, but Christ lives in [us]..." (Gal. 2:20). We are not bound to "conform to the pattern of this world," but we can be "transformed by the renewing of [our] mind[s]" (Rom. 12:2). Everything in us that doubts the goodness of God, everything that is unwilling to love others, everything that fears we will not be loved, has been destroyed in Jesus and the life of God is in us through the Spirit of God so that our freedom does not depend on us, but on God (Rom. 9:16). The work of freedom/transformation/renewal is not our work, but God's effort working in us through Jesus.

It is by our limitation that we can be set free because God has given to us unlimited mercy. If we are willing to give all our sin away, all the shame, all the penalties and all the death that goes along with it, we are given love, honor, blessing, and life in exchange. We just have to give God permission to come and break everything that we have built with our own hands and strength—that is the choice we have been given.

Chapter 12

CHOOSING FREEDOM

WE ALL MAKE CHOICES. EVERY DAY we make hundreds of choices, and we don't even think about most of them. We choose what to wear. We choose what to eat, several times. We choose with whom to speak. At some point, we made certain choices that may limit our current choices: we chose a profession, or at least we chose where to work. We choose to work, or not work. We choose to be parents, or not to be parents.

We can also decide if we are willing to live a life with God where He is completely free to make us free. We can choose to be open to His life or we can choose to close ourselves off from Him. The more freely we allow God to come in, the more places in ourselves we open up, the more He has access to share His life with us. If we are willing, He can show us who He really is. If we choose to restrict ourselves, we will see very little of who He is, or we will not see Him at all. We can choose to separate ourselves from God. That is the choice Adam and Eve made, and we are as free as they were to make that same choice.

God loves us so much that He is willing to risk that we will not come to Him so we understand that we are free. He put everything at risk for the sake of allowing us to have the understanding that we are not obligated. There is nothing that we have to do, but we can choose to do what pleases us. It is what pleases us that God wants to get involved with. He doesn't want to keep us from enjoying life. On the contrary, He created us to enjoy living. However, over time, as a matter of prior choices, or as a result of how we were raised, how we were taught, or what we experienced, we can develop an enjoyment of activities that are not beneficial for us.

Some of the choices we make have become a matter of habit. We made the same choice over a period of time, and it developed a pattern that directs our behavior that looks like it is not chosen, but at some point, we made a choice that led to that pattern. Those choices became ingrained in us and produce a result in keeping with the choice. Certain choices have immediate results while others have results that develop over time. Either way, it becomes cause and effect, not necessarily as a matter of our effort, but because of our choice.

There is a subtle distinction to understand here. God makes it clear that we receive life or death as a result of choice, but in neither case do we receive based on our effort. If our effort could have gained us life, then religion would have been sufficient and there would have been no need for Jesus to surrender His life over to death for our sake. Repeatedly in Scripture, God shows us His pattern for making choices that lead to a life that involves Him, or the pattern prepared for those who do not choose to involve Him. It is a matter of choice and not a matter of effort.

It began with Adam, Eve, and the choice between two trees. They were allowed to choose a life-giving connection to God, who engages us personally and reveals all things to us based on our relationship with Him, or the knowledge of good and evil, our own understanding independent of involvement with God, which leads to death. What is not explained ahead of time is that the ability to see through the self is both extremely limited and is always corrupted by our lack of connection to God. It is only through relationship with God that we can clearly see to make choices that lead to life. This is again shown in the wilderness when the people of Israel are given the Law (Deut. 28). The people of God are given the conditions upon which they can receive life or death, blessings or curses. They are given a choice that leads to a perpetual renewal of life with God, or breaks faith with God by choosing an independent path.

We see this again with the cross and Jesus. We are once again given a choice between life and death. In this case, we have to choose the death of Jesus so that we can engage God in His life. It is a choice that will lead to an unbreakable agreement between man and God called a covenant. A covenant binds the lives of two people into one so that each receives all the benefit, and deficits, from the other. In our relationship with God, we bring our death, and He brings His life. If we are willing to surrender our dead life to be joined with His acceptance of it on the cross, He will surrender His life to us.

We have a choice to come back to God, who places life and death at our feet so we will always know we have a choice. This is the beginning of freedom, and it is a huge key. We have to know that the choice is ours, or it is just another religious activity required by law and not the freedom of a will that is choosing to surrender to love. We have to surrender to love, or nothing God does to us will ever be understood by us as good, or loving. We will never see who He is and what He is doing if we think it is just an exercise on His part to dole out judgment or get His way. God is not looking to judge us, and He is not some child throwing a tantrum just to get his way. He is longing to know us and make Himself known to us. He is passionate to love us and have us fall in love with Him.

In my life, it has been critical for me to understand that the choice I made to surrender to Him was an action made in my will. It is not something I did by myself. He gave me the grace I needed to make the choice, but it was me who lay on the ground and told Him He could have all of me if He would remove the pain that was consuming my being. I chose to exchange the inner pain that was destroying me every day to embrace God, who has spent fifteen years restoring me to a way of making choices through Him; He has done this while removing the consequences of the choices I had made prior to my surrender to Him, and the effects of the choices of my family over many generations that were affecting me every day. He is restoring every blessing that not only I have missed out on, but that my family has missed. He makes all things new! (Rev. 21:5)

It has been critical for me to know it was my choice because sometimes I have needed to remember that God is not punishing me through the difficult circumstances and events that I have sometimes passed through, but rather He gives me opportunities to make choices that lead to different results. He just keeps giving me the chance to choose until I make a choice that connects with who He is and how He and I have joined together. It is a choice that leads me into a deeper union. If it weren't mine, it would not have changed me the same way. I would have stayed at the level of religion and requirement I was at instead of being challenged to make choices that lead to life, but I always have the option to choose Him, or not. We all do.

I also had to know that it was a choice because a lot of what brings relief from pain and destruction is extremely painful itself. To unravel the threads within our lives that try to restrict, or reveal an image that does not reflect the truth, we have to come face to face with the memories, emotions, and at least mentally face the people who have hurt us (or we have hurt) and bring it to the place of death so it can be redeemed. God can bring life to anything, but we have to allow Him to bring up everything that He wants to bring up so it can be faced and dealt with. See, God is not judgmental, but He does need to reveal what is going to be eventually destroyed so it can be removed now. It is better for us if what will be destroyed is removed from us before it destroys everything that it potentially will—especially if that destruction has eternal consequences.

God will reach His hand inside and touch the place that hurts the most. He will press the spot that is bursting with pain. He is not doing this to remind us of the things that have hurt us most, or to provoke guilt over the things we have done that greatly hurt others.

He is not causing pain that is not already there. He is touching broken places to show us that they exist. Most of us are so used to living in pain that we do not know what it is like without it. We have no idea what the absence of pain is like, much less actually being at peace. We cannot relate to a life that is filled with love and joy and freedom. It escapes us because we have no baseline for understanding. It is not relevant in our world. Pain has become the inescapable, ever-present voice that nags at us until we eventually forget it is still speaking.

God is not coming to silence the voice of pain. He has come to reveal the voice of pain so He can remove its words entirely. He is moving us into a place we do not know. We often resist God moving in our lives because we would rather live "safely" in the place we know than risk the possibility of life we have never experienced. We cannot think what it might be, so we reject the possibility of it. Heaven is a good example of this. We have a hard time accepting the notion of heaven because we cannot see it, but the reality of Jesus is that we can experience heaven here on earth, and know it by virtue of His life in us. Jesus, by His nature, is the heaven we are looking for. Relationship with Him makes it real, and His Spirit is the guarantee of that reality overtaking eternity.

The walk that will get us there is extremely personal. This is a choice within us to gain the kingdom of heaven. It is the choice to have God remove in us everything that will not last forever, and allow Him to weave Himself into us. He marries to our created beings His uncreated being. This is through covenant. This is two becoming one. This is renewal. This is the fire of God. The kingdom advances within us as the King of fire advances within us. The deeper within us His reign stretches, the more His life consumes us. The fire of God will destroy everything that cannot exist in heaven. The fire of love will burn into us everything that lasts forever.

Chapter 13

THE BASELINE

T O COME INTO A PLACE OF RENEWAL THAT will fully release the King in our lives, we must face the baselines of how we have lived. We all have baselines from which we operate. We have levels for every aspect of our lives that we have accepted as normal. We have baselines for love and relationship, for driving our cars, for the workplace, for raising children, and on and on. By the time we are adults, most of these are not even on a conscious level of thought, but either influence or completely dictate our everyday living. What I am calling a baseline, or baselines, are basically the beliefs that inform our choices and behavior. These will often be mistaken for our own personality, or we might even believe that they are part of the way we are made. Again, I want to say that God will shake these baselines and beliefs.

When God comes in and lives within us, He begins to challenge the baselines. These baselines often appear as the boundaries we have built around our lives—some useful, some destructive—which we believe are keeping us safe. We believe some things so strongly that we mistake them for our identity when they are just constructs of decisions we have made. God wants to unravel these baselines and create a whole new set of accepted pathways that allow Him to move within our lives.

The problem with our baselines is that they usually restrict our lives more than they keep us safe or help us in any way. Our baselines are frequently created by us as a result of our judgments about a situation, event, or person (people) that we have experienced in our lives. These preconceived notions that are designed to keep harm away are typically only useful for keeping us locked in and God locked out rather than keeping us from being hurt. Often they are keeping hurt that has come into our lives from being released.

I have found in my own life that the more I tried to keep myself from being hurt, the more hurt I became. Judgments create beliefs in us that inform us we are unsafe and they often cause us to build walls around ourselves mentally, emotionally, and spiritually. Many times those judgments are based on hurt to begin with. That hurt is locked into place by the judgment we make, and it becomes part of our baseline. The judgment we make becomes a mental or emotional structure without us even realizing it, and without realizing that it will interfere with the activity of our heart; and, it is the heart that God uses for a doorway into the rest of our being.

It is only through repentance, forgiveness, and the release of our judgmental thoughts that God can remove the walls that keep us from acting in love. God needs us to agree with Him in releasing others from judgment so that He can be free to move in us completely. He will not overrule the freedom of our will to choose or force us to do anything. He simply wants us to choose to accept His purpose for our freedom, and for others to be free. It is God's plan that we all be free. When we choose to judge we actually do not limit the other person's freedom, but we do limit our own, though other people can be horribly affected by our judgments also. If you know how you are affected by the judgments of others, you can understand how others can be affected when you judge them.

Our judgments can bring an end to relationships. When we judge we remove the possibility of restoration. We are placing ourselves in the place of God and attributing a value to an individual based on our perception of their actions. God values people based on their being. He created them and did an amazing job in doing so. He is looking at us as we were made to be, desiring that we be restored to that way of creation. When we take His place in judgment, we devalue His creation and proclaim that we know the truth better than He does. It is also noteworthy that when God comes to administer justice, seated as King in all His authority, He is seated upon the throne of grace (Heb. 4:16). Jesus did not face torture and death to sit in judgment over humanity, but rather to restore life and love to humanity. We could never make a sacrifice more worthy than His that we might hold judgment over those He has forgiven.

We are so often wrong about people and situations for no other reason than our limitations as people to see all paths and all ends. Something usually led someone to a place of sin that we cannot see. Many times, they are not even sinning, but we are offended because of our limited, or skewed, view. God desires to show His compassion to all that He has made, and it is our place to do the same. Judgment tries to defeat God's purpose rather than embrace it because "mercy triumphs over judgment" (James 2:13).

God comes in and shakes our baseline beliefs. He comes to establish a new path to life. He came to break the hold of sin and death, and our judgment can be just as sinful a behavior as every other sin. The constructs we build are just as sinful as the lie someone might tell about us, the curse that they spit in our direction in an angry fit, or the careless and unfaithful act of a good friend. The difference between a single act of sin and the baseline structures that we establish around our lives is that the act of sin from someone else is usually just that—isolated—at least in terms of their effect on us. The broken baselines we live through are often working sin through us all the time.

When we have this kind of judgment in our lives, we are usually unable to act without sinning in the area that structure exists, and we can have many of these. It was a huge revelation for me when I read *The Spiritual Man* by Watchman Nee. This is just a paraphrase of his writing, but what struck me was his explanation of the potentially sinful behavior we can bring forth in our attempts to do "good Christian works." He basically says that any work we perform out of selfish desire, no matter how good the act may externally appear to be, it is sin within us driving the effort. Now this does not mean we should stop doing works of service for the Lord if we do not have an undeniably perfect motive, but it should make us stop and seek the Lord regarding our hearts.

There are many who have appeared to be doing the work of God while building kingdoms to themselves to serve their own image of glory. This is a pitfall set by the devil, and the very work of his own pride and fall from the heavens. We should not live in fear of being like this, but aware that our choices can bend around us if we are not looking into the eyes of God. If we live through our structures rather than through a relationship with the Holy Spirit, we are locked into behavior patterns instead of being free to act in accordance with the often spontaneous and delightful will of God. We are also hindered from acting through His absolute desire for us to love, give, bless, and completely share life with others.

God shakes these baselines so that they will be exposed, and we can face them with Him. He wants to undo what we have done. He is looking to recreate us, to restore us to the way we were originally created. As Christians, we are so often concerned with the outward condition of our behavior that we forget God is more interested in the heart of people. Once the heart is released and revealed to the truth, to be as it was designed to be, the behavior will come into freedom. When we live out of our heart for God, the rest of us will follow. Where the heart goes, the soul and body go.

God makes it plain that His place in the heart is crucial. In Luke and Matthew He explains, "A good man brings good things out of the good stored up in his heart, and the evil man brings evil things out of the evil stored up in his heart..." (Luke 6:45). God promised this to those who place their trust in him: "I will give you a new heart and put a new spirit in you; I will remove from you your heart of stone and give you a heart of flesh. And I will put my Spirit in you and move you to follow my decrees and be careful to keep my laws" (Ezek. 36:26–27).

Jesus never came to remove the Law but to fulfill its purpose in restoring us to God. The Law shows us the consequence of sin, and it sets an example of how to live. It also reveals the inability of our own work and effort to reveal right relationship and behavior in us. Jesus did the exact same thing in his life. He spent three and a half years showing us how to live and died to show us the consequence of sin; He then removed the destructive force of sin for those who invite Him to come and work out His death and resurrection in their lives. He provides right relationship and behavior through his Spirit in us.

Jesus comes and gives us a new spirit. Being born again is the receipt of a new spirit. From there we enter into salvation. His Spirit living in our spirit moves us to follow His example, His decrees, and His will. We enter into His life. He comes into our hearts and the effect is obedience by nature rather than by work. We must realize that this takes time. Paul exhorts us to "only let us live up to what we have already attained" (Phil. 3:16). The divine is as the natural in that a spiritually new-born being is no more mature than a physically newborn baby is. Maturity takes time, discipline, and a great deal of patient love. It is not a sin to take time to grow into maturity: that is the nature of creation.

However, trying to accomplish the work of the Spirit through our own effort is just as much sin as full rebellion to God. Working salvation for ourselves is always sin, even if it looks good on the outside. That is religion, and

Jesus made it plain that He would not accept religion. We are not a substitute for God. Religion is all about replacing God with self. It is a back handed proclamation that we can do in ourselves what He suffered and died to make possible. It is the belief that we can bring forth life out of death. There is only One who has died that was raised from the dead for the sake of all. Once we accept our need of Jesus for salvation, to believe that we can handle the rest of our lives on our own is not only a lie, but it's not even rational to think that way. We are not only saved by grace, but grace is the administration of all life as we grow through our journey with God.

I think it is important to realize that even the Law itself was established in grace. How could it be different? God is gracious and compassionate, abounding in love (Ps. 86:15). Again, the purpose of the Law is to show us both the consequence of sin and the cost of true fellowship. The Law itself is a baseline from which we are supposed to work in grace toward God and each other. Of course, the baseline sinfulness of man could not receive the grace in it, and it was the purpose of God to reveal the baseline of our sinful nature through the Law. The Law reveals the structures within us that do not bring life and goodness the way that his Spirit living in us can. It was God's grace to reveal to us that we were unable to live by grace without His life within us, so that He could come and make all things possible in us.

Chapter 14

EXPOSED BY THE HOLY SPIRIT

OD WANTS TO EXPOSE US. IT IS NOT about embarrassment. It is not about getting into the past for the sake of digging it up, to lay us bear, and leave us there without delivering us. It is not about talking about painful things that you would rather forget, though He will do that. It's getting obstacles out of the way. It's about creating a clear path in which you can walk. John the Baptist reiterates the words of Isaiah, "Make straight the way of the Lord" (John 1:23 and Isa. 40:3). Isaiah goes on to say, "Every valley shall be raised up, every mountain and hill made low; the rough ground shall become level, the rugged places a plain. *And the glory of the Lord will be revealed...*" (Isa. 40:4–5, italics added).

It is about having a place in your heart where He can dwell, where His glory can be revealed in every one of us "...and all mankind together will see it" (Isa. 40:5). If the spaces in our hearts are filled with other things, He is just another outsider to us. He is just another unwelcome visitor. Maybe you're at the door with a shotgun, screaming, *"Get off my lawn, you crazy hippie!"*

I don't know who it really makes you, but I know who it doesn't make you—His. You might have the label on the jar, but the contents are questionable, like an old milk jug filled with gasoline. It will store the gas, but the inside and the outside just don't match. Conveniently, some milk jugs are clear. We are not. We need to choose to be transparent. This is an option for us, for better or for worse, and we get to make the call. God can allow things to get very uncomfortable for us in the hope that we will see the need we have, but the choice to open our lives to Him is ours and ours alone. It is a power beyond imagination, and it is all in our hands.

You hold the keys to eternal life for yourself, and the will to come to Him or stay where you are. If you feel distant from God, it might be because He is moving forward and you are not willing to go. I have been in close relationship with people who refuse to move toward God in His work to reveal the truth of who they are, and I have seen this principle at work in those people: the less you are yourself, the less you are yourself. What I mean by that is, when you are not being who God made you to be, you will make more and more choices that are not in line with your created being. You were made a certain way, for a certain purpose, to be a specific expression of God, and to have a unique relationship with Him that can never be replicated in anyone else, ever. In the history of the world, there has never been another you, and there never will be. You are irreplaceable. When you do not agree with that, it makes a total mess of who you are.

Now, I want to digress for a moment to say I have made a specific point in this book to make little mention of the devil. I have done that for a reason. I believe the devil exists. I believe he is a liar, and the father of all lies (John 8:44). I believe he came to steal, kill, and destroy (John 10:10). I believe he is powerful and has the knowledge of creation because he watched God make the earth (Gen. 1; Ezek. 28:13). I believe he understands the inner workings of man and that he uses that to manipulate and bend things made by God to his corrupted and perverted heart. I also know there are a lot of great books out there that cover the subject of overcoming the devil.

I also believe that for people who have placed their faith in Jesus Christ, he is completely and totally powerless against us unless we give Him the place to use his power. Now I could make all kinds of disclaimers regarding that statement, because I also do not believe it is that black and white. However, I think we frequently give the devil too much credit and do not take the responsibility for our own confused and broken decisions. Sometimes we simply make bad choices, and we need to face up to it and stop pointing fingers, not only at people, but the devil. God overcame. We get to choose to walk with Him in the victory He won for us.

So, back to the exposure thing. If we want to get real with God and have a delightful and intimate relationship with Him, we are going to be exposed. We are going to be uncovered. We are going to be the way we were made—naked. We have to face up to this. We were created without clothes on, completely exposed to God and each other. That was the nature of humanity. However,

God in this day is not looking to physically expose us (so please don't go to your church and strip down naked and say that I said to do it!). He wants to expose the heart. The heart, the inner being, is the goal. That was the plan. He is getting back to the part that died at the time of original sin. He is coming to relate Spirit to spirit. That is where mankind began and where we must begin again. He will do whatever is necessary to reveal us so we can come to Him in spirit and in truth (John 4:23).

God is interested in all our behavior, and it's not because He is looking over our shoulder to see if we are doing something wrong. He is not a schoolteacher with a ruler waiting for us to mess up so He can whack us on the knuckles. He is not an impatient parent waiting to yell at us and whip us with a belt. He is not a harsh speaking, mean faced, grumpy old man sitting up in heaven looking down with disdain.

He is interested in us because He made us, and He is passionate about restoring His creation to its original design—love. Proverbs shows us a picture of the Father and Son creating the world. "Then I [Jesus] was constantly at his [The Father's] side. I was *filled with delight* day after day, *rejoicing* always in his presence, *rejoicing* in his whole world, *and delighting in mankind*" (Prov. 8:30–31, Italics added). He is wanting, delighting, waiting and excited to have us, hold us, kiss us and tell us how amazingly wonderful we are. He is unwaveringly willing to embrace and romance a dirty, rotten-to-the-core, willing to admit that they are furiously angry, sinner. He is willing to stand toe-to-toe with a person who would rather slap somebody than hug them, the type of person who would spit in Jesus' eye for simply looking at them.

What is difficult to deal with is the religious zealot who has the same attitude in his heart as the hateful sinner, but likes to look good to everyone around him, so he masks his true heart with a smile. This difficulty arises not because God loves them less, but because those people don't often see with their hearts, rather, they see with their corrupted "knowledge of good and evil" minds. At the end of the day, the vicious sinner who is willing to confess, and the religious person who looks fantastic on the outside, act the ways they do for the same reasons: they are terrified.

We are all the same. Without God in our innermost parts, we are terrified little kids looking for acceptance. That is the bottom line: we long to be loved, and we do almost anything to hide the fact that that's what we want. We don't want to admit that's what we *need* because we are terrified that we just won't get it. We were made for love. We were created to be loved and to love. We know it deep inside without being told. We know it without thinking about it, just as we know to breathe. It is part of the fabric of our being. We were made for God. We were made for His love to be in us. And we were made to love Him in return with complete freedom, as if rejection didn't even exist, and yet rejection is the very thing we live to avoid. We hide the most vulnerable, most needy places in us, to keep ourselves from being hurt, and the end result is that we really only miss out on love.

In Jesus, rejection does not exist. It is not in His Being. He does not accept lies, or perversion, or manipulation, but He does not reject us as individuals. He has different ways of loving, but no pattern for rejection. He loves the Pharisees in a very different way than He loves adulterers. For the religious, He knows that offending their religious beliefs is the most loving action He could take. He knows that to break down the selfish attitudes of religion He has to present to them a life that is full of understanding and does not negate the Law, but explains the heart of the Law. It is still up to them to see God with their hearts so they can move beyond their selfish desires.

So many times Jesus faced the Pharisees with explanations and answers they were not willing to see. Time and again, Scripture says that the crowds were amazed by His teachings (Matt. 13:54; Mark 1:22; Luke 5:17–26). They acknowledged that they had seen remarkable things (Luke 5:26), but they could not wrap their minds around it enough to let go of their own teachings, which Jesus calls "rules taught by men." Religious people refuse the deepest internal love ever because they insist that what they *know* is better than believing there can be a One and Only truth that is not demanding by its nature. God has not given us the one choice of Jesus as a way to reject everyone who does not believe, but because a true heart of love has to be committed to one love. God is trying earnestly to get to our hearts. For those who insist on understanding everything (as I like to do) it can be difficult to break into the heart. But, Jesus insists on trying over and over to get past the defense system of the mind and speak to the heart. Man was not made for the Sabbath, but the Sabbath for man (Mark 2:27). That is love. If you can hear and understand that real life is not about the external life we see, you have begun to break the hold of religion.

For the adulterer, Jesus gets straight to the heart because people caught sinning need to know they are still accepted. Were there ever more powerful words spoken than, "Then neither do I condemn you...Go now and leave your life of sin" (John 8:11). Jesus speaks to this adulterous woman as a person. I do not condemn *you*. Then He addresses the action He must reject. She is accepted, and the sin is rejected. That is love. That is freedom because our identity is not in what we do, but who He says we are.

Naming something we do as sin is not rejection unless we have built our identity on our actions. If who we are is completely based on what we do, we will believe that to reject a sin in our lives is to reject us as a person. But if we believe that we are identified by our relationship with God, accepted based on His love and desire, restored based on the identity and actions of Jesus, then we understand that our sin and who God sees are not the same. Paul says this about sin: "As it is, it is no longer I myself who do it [sin], but it is sin living in me. For I know that nothing good lives in me, that is, in my sinful nature..." (Rom. 7:17–18). Sin is not who we are but what comes out of us when our heart is not given over to God.

I know for myself many of my past sin patterns were very external. They were not hidden sins, quiet and unnoticed, but very open and apparent. Some people in my life chose to speak to those sins with hardness and bitterness. It made me strive to look better on the outside, to change my behavior, to be a "better" person, but trying to deal with it that way really didn't change me internally. The broken heart and wrong thinking were not healed and transformed. I made efforts so I would not be rejected by those who did not approve of me, but none of my efforts was bringing the transformation that love establishes so freely.

Over time, those who offered me sincere and consistent acceptance despite my very apparent failures won my heart, and the much-needed change happened. Love changed me when I could not. Trying to change just made me angry, frustrated, and fueled feelings of isolation and depression. Jesus is the most consistent person in this effort of love. He is the One who showed me that what other people in my life were doing was offering His acceptance and mercy.

Jesus was offering Himself in vulnerability without me being right. He didn't ask me to be safe or nice. He didn't expect me to understand things I had never been taught. He just smiled at me when I was seething. He looked at me patiently when I let my emotions get the better of me. When I was ready to see His laughing at me as love, He started laughing about my behavior to let me know how ridiculous I was being sometimes. He never asked me to be better than I was. He allowed me to be me—venomous, toxic, and full of bitter rage. He exposed my judgmental and vicious heart that was ready to punish people for any slight. I was an inner tyrant who went to church with a smile and did anything they asked me to so I would not be judged and rejected. I prayed, played worship songs, and preached the gospel. And I hated myself more than I hated everybody else.

What I am saying is that this was in my heart, mingled with the good I desired to do. I loved God and wanted to do all things well for Him. I just had no idea where I stood at any given moment. I was trying to love from a place of total fear. He was trying to reveal that fear and show me that He was exposing it so I could agree to let Him take it away.

I was supremely insecure about my every action, and ultimately about my very existence. Was it good enough? Did I pray long enough? Did I pray too long? Did I say the wrong thing? Was that Biblical? Does my pastor like me? Do my friends really like me? Am I okay? Will I ever be okay? Did I do that wrong? Am I right? Do I even belong here? Why am I alive?

Then Jesus simply came to me, saying, "Give it all to me. I don't want all your efforts. I want you. That is who you are right now, and I want *you*. I accept *you*. I see past all the garbage you have covered yourself with to protect your broken heart. You can let it go. I want it. When you are ready to let it go, I am here. I will take it away. I will wash you off. I have paid for you to come. It is done. You are worth it. You are. You. Worth it. You. Is that okay? Is it okay to be worth it now? I am here. Come now."

He does it all. He opens the way to change. He takes it all—everything I could never perfect, or deal with, or be rid of myself. He takes it as easily as I would if I was taking the trash out to the curb. And it's gone. It's not that I have it under control. It's just not there, as if it never existed. Acceptance does all that. Love moves it out. The same love that made me, restores me. The same hands that formed me from dirt, that gripped nails and blood, are the hands that welcome me home. He welcomes me in when I will not welcome myself, because I welcomed Him when I couldn't welcome anyone else. When I was terrified, He came with love because "perfect love drives out fear" (1 John 4:18).

He lays me bare. We have walked together in this for over fifteen years, and He will continue to walk with me. He will always bring me to a place where He gets to show me His love. He is always looking to share Himself with me, to show me who I am. He shows me who others are to Him as well. He loves them, too. He loves, loves, and never stops loving. And while I don't need to try to save the world, and help every person I see, because I am just not able, I want to help who I can. I want to give to the people He has given me to give to. I want to live a life that gives where He says, "There!" I want to see the ways He sees so when He offers a solution, I can be there with Him. His love is for every one of us. He is for every one of us.

This is the promise: "But if we walk in the light, as he is in the light, we have fellowship with one another, and the blood of Jesus, his Son, purifies us from all sin" (1 John 1:7). Again, it comes back to both our life in Jesus and the life we choose with each other. It is only through fellowship, life with one another, that we get the fullness of who we are. We can only be totally ourselves, totally true, by being in relationship with each other. Just as much as we were made for God, we were made to be with one another.

It is in seeing each other, loving each other, and honestly bearing with one another in love that we come to understand the fullness of freedom. If we do not come to each other in this way, we are destined to lose ourselves, each other, and miss the opportunity to see God for all He is. Just as much as we are each a unique expression of God, made for His pleasure, we each see God differently. We see through our own experiences, and we miss out if we do not choose to see others, and see God, through His eyes. Everyone is unique and each life is special because we are created by God and connected to God. Even disconnected from God, we are amazing because we are still created by Him.

Chapter 15

ENGAGING LOVE

L OVE BREAKS THROUGH THE DARKNESS OF life like nothing else can. The mind enjoys the challenge of developing new thoughts and working out a problem. The body finds fulfillment in engaging in the physically tangible world in which we live. The spirit longs to be engaged in relationship with God. The heart wants to be engaged completely by love.

Many might consider this overly romantic, or an oversimplification, but perhaps that is in the way we define love. Love has many forms and faces, many ways of touching, and is powerful beyond measure. It is so much more than a kiss, or a hand held, although those physical experiences can be exceptionally powerful. It is more than the words we speak of kindness, or understanding, or desire. It is more passionate even than a sacrificial action or willingness to yield in the face of another, even more than the surrender possible in the place of complete vulnerability before another. Love, as I have known it, will destroy false realities and build all new worlds. It is a place where death cannot think to be, where dreams go to dream even bigger, and breath comes short but full of life. It defines life and each one of us. And what we accept as love will become the reality we accept. There is nothing that can overcome the way love can. The key is knowing love, accepting love, and allowing love to be as it is without trying to change it. To be clear, we must understand that God is love and by His very nature He is defining us through His interaction with us. God came to show us the true nature of love and to establish Himself in us.

Now I could dole out all of the great scriptures concerning love, of which there are many, but I think it makes sense to start with a story. When I came to the Lord, it was an unbearably hot summer day before my senior year in college. I was deep into the idea of myself, full of college level genius just waiting to bloom into a supernova, and on a journey that would eventually burn me out completely. I was overheating and ready to explode. I could not mentally or emotionally hold my life together anymore. This was caused in part by how out of order my mind and spirit were to the way God had created me. Another factor in this was my loving Creator's application of pressure to the faulty work of the life I had been building. I had come to despair of the future that I had. Despite being very intelligent, successful as a student, and a hard working young man, I had no hope that my future would be a good one. This again was a duality: part of it was my own darkened thinking and part was God revealing to me the bleak reality of a life lived without Him.

Other than my intellectual pursuits was my constant pursuit of women. I slipped too easily from one companion to another, never comfortable within myself and never satisfied with them. I will also say that my decision-making skills were without wisdom, and the women I was choosing were not usually looking for a reciprocal investment. Waking up in the same bed with someone the morning after you first meet is really not an indicator of a relationship destined for life-long commitment and unconditional love. And that was really about all I was good at in relationships. I could make a woman feel great for a little while, but I did not know how to see the whole of a woman, just as I did not expect someone to see the whole me.

Many years later, after many years of marriage, and the failure of that marriage, I understand that no person can really attend to the whole of anyone else. There is no complete fulfillment in even the best relationship between a man and woman, and that is because we were created first for God and then for each other. Where we get lost so often is looking for more than we can gain through other people. I also believe we can get lost looking for everything from God when we were in fact made to interact with others. We were not made to be separated from God, and neither were we made to be isolated from one another. We *need* both relationships to be a complete human being.

It is the joint experience of both God's love and the interactive love of relationships in our daily lives that move our heart to the place it was made to be. We come to the fullness of expression through both types of love pouring into our lives. We were not created to relate solely to God, and we were not designed to relate solely to man. There is a great deal of teaching and expression being given to the idea that God is to be our everything, but this was not what God intended. If we were meant to have relationship only with God, why do the Ten Commandments have four commands concerning the Lord and six concerning our fellow man? If we were made to relate to and depend solely on God, why did God go to such lengths to create from the one man, male and female? Why was creation "good" when the only possible relationship was between God and man, but "very good" when the human relationship began? What kind of relationship would you have with your spouse, or a child with their parents, if there was no dependency in the relationship?

There are aspects of our nature that cannot be fulfilled by anyone other than God, and needs that cannot be met by anyone other than Him. Yet, there are needs that cannot be met by God for which He planned and attended to the desires we have been given: a passion for a good work, a delight in sexual intimacy, the enjoyment of a good meal. The fact that we were created with a physical nature and not just a spiritual nature shows that we need the interaction of those around us. That Jesus came in the nature of a man is testimony to our need to interact physically. It is through the complete relationship of God and man interacting with us that we become complete.

Scripture says to love your neighbor as yourself. To do to others as we would have done for us. I think it is a reality that we will not do otherwise. And here is what I mean: we are not able to love others any better than we love ourselves. We cannot be more patient with someone else than we can be with ourselves. We cannot be more generous with others than we can be with ourselves. Maybe we will attain to it in the short term, but not in the length and breadth of an ongoing relationship. I can certainly be enough like Jesus to give some money to the homeless person on the street, or even take the time to bring him to a restaurant and buy him a meal, but would I treat him like my brother? I will admit that I am not there yet in love. I would like to be one day, but I have not arrived at that kind of love yet.

What that means is that I would not take myself in were I out on the street. I would leave myself on the street in that situation. I would reject myself because I did not have my life together better than that. I would be afraid of what I would steal from me if I let myself in my house. Would I hurt myself, or more specifically my family, if I invited homeless me into my house? These would be the things I would think about in terms of a homeless person coming into my home. And, of course, we need to be wise when it comes to who we invite into our homes, but this is a heart check question. Even if we can't bring someone into our home, what can we do? We can certainly do better than a dollar! This is why we need to have love come in and change us. We need to see how lovable we are, how we were made for love, how God planned to have good done toward us. He would, and did, take us in off the street and into His home. If we are worth it to Him, why are we not worth more to ourselves?

This is not about selfish love that does for ourselves. It is not about, "I love myself, so I bought myself a BMW."

(I have no problem with owning BMWs—not a sin) But it is about, why I bought the BMW. Was I trying to fill a need? Was I trying to plug a gap in my self-worth? It doesn't work. It may for a time, but get a scratch on that Beemer and see if you don't feel like God wasn't looking out for you. The heart will betray the truth of the love within. Our actions tell us where we are. They are informants. The inner actions, the thoughts and beliefs that only you and God see are the worst informants of all. Secret little spies looking at everything that we *would* do, but are too afraid to let anyone see.

Well, God already knows. The real secret that will set us free is believing that, since He knows, we might as well talk it out with Him and let Him love us through it. Whatever is needed to be free of those things within us that are not of love, He is willing and able to do. God can be trusted. God is safe. All He wants is to help you. To help me. To make a life with us. He wants us to tell Him the bad things, the secret things, the dark things. He wants to bring Himself into everything that we cannot accept about ourselves, accept about others, and especially the things we cannot accept about Him.

Many years ago, God taught me something that changed the way I looked at love, and it set me free to see Him as He is. That truth has changed everything. For a long time I looked at God through my definition of love. I gauged Him through my understanding of love. I thought He was a tough God. Honestly, I thought He was a brute. For a while, it just made sense to me. God was tough, firm, but wanted good for me. I honestly spent a lot of time being really angry at Him because I felt like I was being abused and taken advantage of.

The reality is that I saw love as tough and hard. I felt often taken advantage of by those who cared about me. This is how I perceived love. God showed me that I needed to redefine love. What He showed me was that I needed to see what He was doing and call *that* love. I had to trust that whatever I knew to be God acting was what love really was, and then try to understand how. He spent years, and is still spending time, breaking down what I believe love to be, and redefining love through His actions toward me. He is showing me the truth about love through my relationship with Him. He is revealing His love for me, not through teaching, not through religious discipline, and not through all the work I do. He is revealing the truth about love through the touch of His Spirit when I am hurting, through the feel of His eyes on me when I am believing I am a failure, and through His speaking to me. He is revealing love through others around me who show me love, who accept me as I am, who really want to see me be myself, who are willing to tell me that I am worth more than I think, and who confront sin in me with patience and by offering their strength to my weakness.

We must do this not only for ourselves, but for each other. We must learn to love. God will show us. God will move us, touch us, seek us, be kind to us, be diligent with us, and never stop. Never. Never. Never. He will always love. He will always tell us that we are worth more. He will also tell us when we are wrong, but He will do it with gentle correction. If He needs to be tough, it is so that

He can show us how to move into something more life-giving, more joyful, and full of promise—never bullying. Being wrong can be one of the best ways to get free, so long as we are willing to become free from it.

We have to choose to look past the mess we have made of ourselves, that others have helped to make, and the messes that others are. We do not accept the sins, but the people. Some people are harder to get through to than others, and some may seem impossible to get through to at all, but God can do anything. It is just a matter of us letting Him do anything. No one can limit God the way we can. But we also get to welcome Him to be completely Himself in our lives. All I can say is, "Wow! Yeah! God being God. Look out, it's gonna get good around here!"

Chapter 16

ACCESS TO GOD

EVERYTHING GOD DOES IS ABOUT HAVING access to Him. It is about getting face to face with Him. The whole purpose for creating man, of Jesus walking on the earth, His being crucified and resurrected, and everything else that is written in Scripture is done for the purpose of bringing man to God. It is about relationship, and we have access to God through our faith in Him.

Before the Law ever came into being there were men and women who experienced God by faith. We look to those like Noah, Abraham, Sarah, and Moses who came face to face with God through their willingness to draw near to Him and hear His voice. They risked everything in their lives on His words. They chose to believe God, and by their faith, they were brought into relationship with God.

Then came the Law. What we have been shown through the Law is the purpose of God to restore us. He shows us how unending our sin is, and how we can never be cleansed from it by the effort of sacrifices made by our own hands, even when it is done so in accordance with His commands. The Law stands to show us that we

cannot, through any effort, have the life God has prepared for us apart from Him. We cannot come into fellowship with Him through any sacrifice or effort we make.
We cannot undo the work of sin in ourselves through any
work we can accomplish (See Hebrews 9 and 10 for a brief
explanation).

The only work that brings us face to face with God is
His. That is the work of the Spirit, the life of God in us,
that makes all the difference. By the Spirit living in us
we become the earthly tabernacle, the earthly dwelling
place of God, and in that way we gain full access to all
of God. In that way, by our willingness to choose Him by
faith, He gives us everything. He comes and lives with us.

Jesus makes it safe for us to be completely honest. He
makes a place within us of perfect safety that allows us
to say whatever we need to, to confess whatever we need
to. He exposes us for our own sake, but He also makes a
place where we can expose ourselves to him. He delights
in hearing our voices, our words, even if they aren't beautiful and lovely words filled with love. He says, "...Show
me your face, let me hear your voice; for your voice is
sweet, and your face is lovely" (Song of Sol. 2:14). If we
are bitter and filled with pain, we can bring it to Him.
If we are full of rage that cannot be contained, we can
bring it to Him. It is better that we take our sins to Him,
that we let them loose on Him if need be so that we can
face the reality of their existence, than to hold it in and
destroy ourselves or behave destructively toward others.

God can take whatever we dish out. He can let it go
and release us from our sin. He already showed us that
when He said, "Father, forgive them, for they do not

know what they are doing" (Luke 23:34). He faced the worst of all of our sins and looked at us with compassion and love. He took all of our sin. His body broke for our sin. He breathed out a faint whisper that said, "It is done." It cannot be undone. We cannot do more than what was done; we cannot sin beyond the measure of what He did for us. There is no depth to which we can sink where He did not go, will not go, will not touch us, hold us, embrace us. We cannot go beyond Him.

But we can ignore Him, overlook Him, stay silent and not let Him into the place where He wants to live. We can deny Him access to ourselves. The greater challenge for us, as fallen people, even those who have turned their lives over to Him, is to let Him have full access to every part of them. We have to choose, one step at a time, day after day, to allow Him to enter every place He asks us to let Him go. We can say, "No," but we will face the loss of His life in that area. By denying God full freedom to all that is in us, we will face some loss of ourselves, some loss of Him, and all the love that comes with Him. We will face the potential loss of some connection that we might have had with the others around us. We are not alone, but the more we act like it, the greater the loss. We cannot selfishly believe that this is all about us. He is risking everything on us coming through so that His Life will be fully revealed in everyone.

We have a life to live with God, and He is ever so willing to live with us. He certainly paid enough to gain access to every part of us. He has the highest level of clearance, but we so often act like if we keep our sins and weaknesses top secret, He will never know or notice that they are there. We try to overlook our sins as we think He will. He doesn't overlook. He removes. He redeems. He restores. He renovates.

The truth of it all is that God is after a people that will simply enjoy him. That's what it's all about. Surrender is all about enjoying God and everything that He enjoys. In England, in 1646, the church tried to make understanding relationship with God as simple as possible because many people were unable to read. So they created the Westminster Shorter Catechism, which says, "Man's chief end is to glorify God, and to enjoy Him forever." I love this. What could be better than enjoying someone forever?

Enjoying forever. Just think about that. Is there insecurity in enjoyment? Is there fear of any kind? Is there sin? Is there pain? Is there any kind of difficulty in any way in a life filled with enjoyment? The point is that enjoyment, though often overlooked in our daily relationships because of all the effort we are putting into them, is the whole point of this thing called life. The whole point of being here on earth is enjoyment. Pleasure is at the right hand of God forever (Ps. 16:11). We are made for enjoyment, made for love, made for peace and joy and singing and dancing. It all seems so frivolous, but aren't these the things that we really live for?

Even those that don't know God look for pleasure and enjoyment. Isn't this the hunger of humanity? So why is it that as friends of God, we look to work so hard? I have no desire to promote a life that is unintentional and full of waste; but shouldn't our actions and the things we do to demonstrate our love for God be more in keeping with who He is, rather than such continual and ongoing efforts? Never ending efforts. This was not what God intended. Why can't we be intentional about enjoying the life of God in us, and in others, and even God Himself?

Unfortunately, so much of what we do in our Christian lives revolves around trying *not* to sin. We are working on not sinning. We try and try and try not to lust. We try so hard not to be angry. We make such an overwhelming effort not to speak coarse words. We just about break the blood vessels in our foreheads trying not to want the things we want that we...just...should...not...want. Ugh! It is so much work. And we fail miserably because God in us is not interested in us working so that we get to the point of merely *not* sinning—not sinning is about as low a mark as we can get when the God of all creation lives in us. When He sees us, He is not even looking at our sin anymore because Jesus has done away with sin and death. He is interested in us living.

God is moving in us with the power of the Spirit to live. He is focused on life, and life has no sin in it. Sin and life never exist together. Only sin and death go together. Life goes along with more life. Sin yields death. Life yields more life. Our spirits have been handed over to life in Jesus! That is the gift that comes to live in us through our simple, little faith. Our little mustard seed of faith invites the greatest life ever thought of.

SIMPLY GOD

FTER ADAM AND EVE HAD EATEN THE fruit they were commanded not to, God came to the garden. "The man and his wife heard the sound of the Lord God as he was walking in the garden in the cool of the day..." (Gen. 3:8). I believe it was God's habit to come and walk with them every day. He does the same with us now, so why would He be otherwise with them? On that day, the man and woman had sinned, covered themselves with fig leaves, and hidden from God. God, knowing full well that they had chosen contrary to His word, still came to walk with them. He did not come full of rage at their sin. He did not come to deliver His judgment against them. He came walking in the garden, looking for them. He came calling out to them, "Where are you?" God is calling out to us today, longing to draw us out of hiding, to walk with us in the cool of day.

God's love is searching us out. He is forever looking for us, longing to find the one He created for love. I want God's love for us to be an ongoing revelation that "neither death nor life, neither angels nor demons, neither the present nor the future, nor any powers, neither height nor depth, nor anything else in all creation, will be able to separate us from the love of God that is in Christ Jesus our Lord" (Rom. 8:38–39). The life we are looking for, if we really want to find God and see Him as He is, requires all of us to surrender every speck of the dust we were made from to the love of God. Through this, we can be restored to a life of walking in the cool of the day with Him and each other. We have to accept the blood, pick up our cross, desire the power of the resurrection, and do it all face to face with Jesus. We cannot get it in our own way or through our own strength, but through revelation. There is no conclusion here, no tidy ending, but a lifetime journey walking with God. It is up to God to reveal Himself. It is up to us to let Him.

ABOUT THE AUTHOR

SEAN HARVEY DEDICATED HIS LIFE TO THE Lord in 1999. After spending several intense years in training with healing and deliverance teams, he found himself working with church leadership in a variety of ministries that eventually revealed a passion for discipleship. Over the years, it has become Sean's defining passion to help others find their life fully revealed in Jesus, and walk in the full manifestation of His character and destiny for them. Sean and his wife, Jessica, currently live in Enfield, CT with their new daughter, Sarah Grace.

CONTACT THE AUTHOR

You may contact Sean Harvey at
formedinsecret@gmail.com.